GW00381717

IMAGES OF SPORT

ASTON VILLA
FOOTBALL CLUB

IMAGES OF SPORT

ASTON VILLA
FOOTBALL CLUB

TONY MATTHEWS

TEMPUS

Frontispiece: Delighted Villa fans celebrate winning the Football
League title in 1981 – the club's first such success in 71 years.

First published 2003

Tempus Publishing Limited
The Mill, Brimscombe Port,
Stroud, Gloucestershire, GL5 2QG
www.tempus-publishing.com

© Tony Matthews, 2003

The right of Tony Matthews to be identified as the Author
of this work has been asserted in accordance with the
Copyrights, Designs and Patents Act 1988.

All rights reserved. No part of this book may be reprinted
or reproduced or utilised in any form or by any electronic,
mechanical or other means, now known or hereafter invented,
including photocopying and recording, or in any information
storage or retrieval system, without the permission in writing
from the Publishers.

British Library Cataloguing in Publication Data.
A catalogue record for this book is available from the British Library.

ISBN 0 7524 3123 4

Typesetting and origination by Tempus Publishing Limited.
Printed in Great Britain by Midway Colour Print, Wiltshire.

Contents

Acknowledgements

I would like to thank James Howarth of Tempus Publishing for agreeing to produce this book. I would also like to thank the FA and the Football League; Adrian Faber (picture editor, *Wolverhampton Express & Star*); the picture library of the *Birmingham Post & Mail*; ex-players Derek Dougan, Jimmy Dugdale, the late Trevor Hockey and Dave Walsh; Grimsby Town and Stoke City Football Clubs; Messrs Brown, Barnes & Bell (photographers of Liverpool); Russell & Sons (Liverpool); Bowden Brothers (London); Andrew Gatt, George Herringshaw, Keith Warsop, John Smith, Reg Thacker, Barry Marsh, Laurie Rampling, Henry Langton and John F. Winder (Bolton). Also, prior to his death in 2002, the cartoonist Norman Edwards granted me permission to utilise some of his excellent caricature drawings of older Villa players.

Several of the photographs used in this book are from my own personal collection, from past and present supporters, families of ex-players, old, defunct newspaper libraries and various other sources. However, in some instances there was no indication as to who owns the copyright of certain pictures (no clear stamp or marking on the back), and therefore I would be pleased to hear from anyone whose copyright has been unintentionally infringed, so that we may include the appropriate acknowledgement in any subsequent edition of this book.

Bibliography

I have referred to several books, some appertaining to the club, to check and re-check certain information, and these include:

Betts, Graham, *The Villans - Day By Day Life At Villa Park*, 1998
Hugman, Barry, *The PFA Premier & Football League Players' Records: 1946-1998*, 1998
Inglis, Simon, *The Football Grounds of Great Britain*, 1987
Johnson, Ian, *The Aston Villa Story*, 1981
Joyce, Michael, *Football League Players' Records: 1888 to 1939*, 2002
Morris, Peter, *Aston Villa: The History of a Great Football Club*, 1960
Several club *Complete Records, Who's Who* publications, and histories.

Introduction

It was once said that the early players of Aston Villa Football Club were a classic example of the nineteenth-century age of 'Muscular Christianity', leading their lives with a Bible in one hand and a football in the other. It is thought that four members of the Wesleyan Chapel cricket team – Jack Hughes, Frederick Matthews, Walter Price and William Scattergood – probably formed the club in 1874 after meeting under a dimly-lit gas lamp on the corner of Heathfield Road and Lozells Road, near to the site of the old Villa Cross public house and opposite the former Wesleyan Chapel (also known as the Aston Villa Church). They agreed, unanimously, to call their football team Aston Villa Wesleyan FC – 'Aston Villa' coming from a large mansion-style dwelling of that name in the locality, or possibly the church. A committee was elected and a fixture list drawn up, with games arranged against teams from Perry Barr, Lozells, Aston, Handsworth, Smethwick, West Bromwich, Tipton and Hagley. In no time at all, the Villa players were up and running – and to a certain extent they haven't stopped!

Things developed quickly and Aston Villa was soon a club strong in all departments, especially on the field of play. The FA Cup was won and then, thanks to Scotsman William McGregor, League football arrived. The Villa quickly added the Championship of that competition to their list of achievements, whilst also collecting various local domestic prizes. They then moved grounds, taking up residence at Villa Park in 1897 – the same year that the team completed the League and FA Cup double. Further League triumphs and FA Cup glory followed as the seasons rolled by, until relegation from the top flight was suffered for the first time in 1936, and after gaining promotion in the 1937/38 season, the Second World War interrupted proceedings.

There was then a barren patch until 1957, when, for the seventh and last time so far, Villa lifted the FA Cup. Four years later, victory was achieved in the inaugural League Cup competition. Demotion from the First to the Third Division and promotion back up again preceded two further triumphs in the League Cup, until, in 1981, Villa won their seventh Football League title. They followed this up by lifting the coveted European Cup and then the Super Cup, later claiming two more League Cup final victories in the 1990s.

Many great players have served the club over the years – far too many to list individually. There have been gifted managers, too, who have guided the team to success and sometimes failure! And, of course, there have been the other members of Aston Villa FC who, over the years, have done extraordinary things to keep the club going. Villa – founder members of the Football League and the Premiership – are, without doubt, one of the great clubs in the world, capable of averaging over 40,000 spectators at home games. Villa Park is now regarded as one of the top six grounds in the country, regularly staging FA Cup semi-finals and the odd international match. Some of the great deeds and some of the important images of the club are recorded in the pages of this book. Enjoy them to the full ... many more will follow.

Tony Matthews
October 2003

Roll of Honour

FA Premiership: runners-up: 1992/93

Football League: Division One Champions – 1893/94, 1895/96, 1896/97, 1898/99, 1899/1900, 1009/10, 1980/81; runners-up – 1888/89, 1902/03, 1907/08, 1910/11, 1912/13, 1913/14, 1930/31, 1932/33, 1989/90

Division Two Champions – 1937/38, 1959/60; runners-up – 1974/75, 1987/88

Division Three Champions – 1971/72

FA Cup: winners 1887, 1895, 1897, 1905, 1913, 1920, 1957; runners-up 1892, 1924, 2000

Double winners (League and FA Cup): 1896/97

League Cup: winners 1961, 1975, 1977, 1994, 1996; runners-up 1963, 1971

European Cup: winners 1982

European Super Cup: winners 1982

Zenith Data Systems Cup Northern Final: runners-up 1990

FA Charity Shield winners: 1981 (shared with Tottenham Hotspur); runners-up 1910, 1957, 1972

Sheriff of London Charity Shield: winners 1899 (shared with Queen's Park), 1901; runners-up 1900

Lord Mayor of Birmingham Charity Cup: winners 28 times (also six finals shared); runners-up 10 times.

Birmingham & District League: winners 1942

Birmingham Senior Cup: winners 17 times, runners-up 9 times

Birmingham League Cup: winners 1942

Football League South: runners-up 1945/46

Wartime Football League North Cup: winners 1944; runners-up 1943

Keys Cup: winners 1942

FA Youth Cup: winners 1972, 1980, 2002; runners-up 1978

Central/Pontins League: champions 3 times; runners-up six times

one

The Early Days

For the first ten years of their existence (1874-84), Aston Villa fulfilled more than 200 fixtures at senior level, their first game being a fourteen-a-side friendly encounter against Aston Park Unity, staged in Aston Park, in January 1875. Although the final score was not recorded, Villa 'lost a closely fought contest', possibly by a goal (or two) to nil.

Two months later, a fifteen-a-side match took place on waste ground in Wilson Road, Aston. Rugby rules were applied in the first half and soccer rules in the second, and it was Villa who came out on top, beating Aston Brook St Mary's Rugby Club 1-0, Jack Hughes scoring what is believed to have been the club's first goal.

Performances got better, top quality players were recruited and, in 1879, Villa entered the FA Cup, defeating Stafford Road (Wolverhampton) 3-2 in a replay after a 1-1 draw in the first round. Then, for reasons unknown, Villa – after being drawn against one of the top sides in the country, Oxford University – pulled out of the competition.

But they had made a start, and thereafter looked forward each season to taking part in this competition and won it for the first time in 1887, beating West Bromwich Albion 2-0 in the final at The Oval. A year later League football was introduced, Villa being one of the twelve founder members, and they did well, finishing as runners-up to double-winning Preston North End in 1888/89. Crowds were getting bigger and the good results matched the team's encouraging performances.

Above left: Jack Hughes, scorer of Villa's first-ever goal in a 1-0 friendly win over Aston St Mary's.

Above right: Arthur Brown was one of Villa's first quality goalscorers. He joined the club in 1880 and stayed for six years, during which time he notched at least 100 goals (in various games), including 15 in 22 FA Cup matches. He also scored four times on his international debut for England in a 13-0 win over Ireland in 1882 (his club colleague Howard Vaughton claimed five).

Opposite below: A matchday card issued for the 1890 Birmingham Senior Cup final between Aston Villa and West Bromwich Albion (a game Villa won 2-0) with the list of fixtures for the following season.

Above: In season 1889/90, Villa finished a moderate eighth in the League table and were knocked out of the FA Cup by Notts County in the second round. However, they did win the Birmingham Senior Cup (beating rivals West Bromwich Albion 2-0 in the final) and the Lord Mayor of Birmingham Charity Cup (defeating Wolves 2-1 in the final). Most of the players who triumphed in those two finals are featured here. From left to right, back row (in kit): Albert Brown, Albert Allen, Jimmy Warner (goalkeeper), Albert Aldridge, Dennis Hodgetts. Front row (seated): Billy Dickson, Fred Dawson, Archie Hunter (ball at feet), Tom Clarkson, Gersom Cox. Seated on ground: John Burton. The gentleman in the back row with the impressive beard (looking right) is William McGregor, founder of the Football League.

Aston Villa Football Club.

OFFICIAL FIXTURES, RESULTS, AND NAMES OF PLAYERS.

West Bromwich Albion v. Aston Villa.

AT PERRY BARR, MAY 24th, 1890.

WEST BROMWICH ALBION.

Umpire:—Mr. W. BISSEKER.   Colours—Blue and White Stripes.

READER.

	GREEN.		POWELL.	
E. HORTON.	C. PERRY.	WILSON.
NICHOLLS.		WHEELDON.
BASSETT.	WOODHALL.	MARSHALL.

J. MARGOSCHIS Agent for MITCHELL'S CELEBRATED ALES.
147, Constitution Hill, Birmingham.

ASTON VILLA.

D. HODGETTS.	W. DICKSON.	A. BROWN.
	McKNIGHT.	A. ALLEN.	
J. BURTON.	J. COWAN.	H. DEVEY.
	G. COX (Capt).	A. ALDRIDGE.	
	J. WARNER.	

ONE PENNY.   Colours Sky Blue and Claret.

J. W. GILL, Printer and Lithographer, Engine Works, Hall Street, Birmingham.

ASTON VILLA

LEAGUE MATCHES,

1890-91.

Date	Club	Where played
Sept. 6	Wolverhampton Wanderers	Wolverhampton.
„ 13	Notts County	Perry Barr
„ 20	Burnley	Burnley
„ 27	West Bromwich Albion	Perry Barr
Oct. 2	Bolton Wanderers	Bolton
„ 11	Everton	Perry Barr.
„ 18	Derby County	Derby
„ 25	Derby County	Perry Barr.
Nov. 1	West Bromwich Albion	West Bromwich
„ 8	Burnley	Perry Barr
„ 15	Accrington	Perry Barr
„ 22	Bolton Wanderers	Perry Barr
„ 29	Notts County	Nottingham
Dec. 6	Blackburn Rovers	Blackburn
„ 13	Blackburn Rovers	Perry Barr
„ 20	Accrington	Accrington
„ 26	Sunderland	Perry Barr
1891.		
Jany. 1	Everton	Everton
„ 3	Preston North End	Perry Barr
„ 10	Sunderland	Sunderland
„ 24	Preston North End	Preston
March 7	Wolverhampton Wanderers	Perry Barr

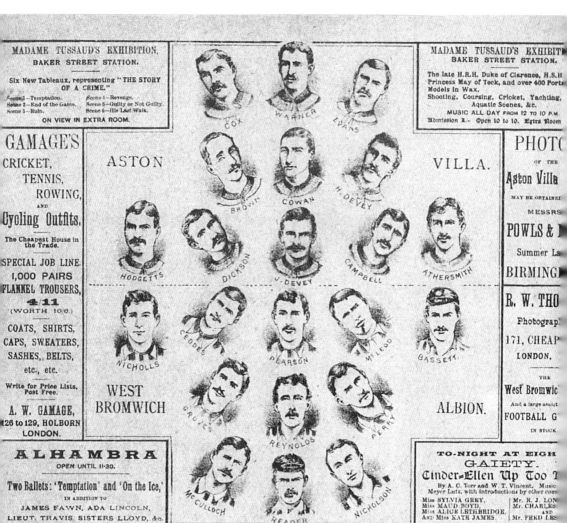

MADAME TUSSAUD'S EXHIBITION,
BAKER STREET STATION.

Six New Tableaux, representing "THE STORY
OF A CRIME."

Scene 1—Temptation.   Scene 4—Revenge.
Scene 2—End of the Game. Scene 5—Guilty or Not Guilty.
Scene 3—Ruin.   Scene 6—His Last Walk.

ON VIEW IN EXTRA ROOM.

MADAME TUSSAUD'S EXHIBIT
BAKER STREET STATION.

The late H.R.H. the Duke of Clarence, H.S.H
Princess May of Teck, and over 400 Port
Models in Wax.
Shooting, Coursing, Cricket, Yachting,
Aquatic Scenes, &c.

MUSIC ALL DAY FROM 12 TO 10 P.M.

Admission 1.- Open 10 to 10. Extra Room

GAMAGE'S
CRICKET,
TENNIS,
ROWING,
AND
Cycling Outfits.
The Cheapest House in
the Trade.

SPECIAL JOB LINE,
1,000 PAIRS
FLANNEL TROUSERS,
4/11
(WORTH 10/6.)

COATS, SHIRTS,
CAPS, SWEATERS,
SASHES, BELTS,
etc., etc.

Write for Price Lists,
Post Free.

A. W. GAMAGE,
126 to 129, HOLBORN
LONDON.

PHOTC
OF THE
Aston Villa
MAY BE OBTAINE

MESSRS

POWLS &

Summer La

BIRMING

R. W. THO
Photograp

171, CHEAP
LONDON,

THE
West Bromwic
And a large assort
FOOTBALL G
IN STOCK

ALHAMBRA
OPEN UNTIL 11-30.

Two Ballets: 'Temptation' and 'On the Ice,'
IN ADDITION TO
JAMES FAWN, ADA LINCOLN,
LIEUT. TRAVIS, SISTERS LLOYD, &c.

TO-NIGHT AT EIGH
GAIETY.
Cinder=Ellen Up Too 1
By A. C. Torr and W. T. Vincent. Music
Meyer Lutz, with introductions by other com

Miss SYLVIA GREY. | Mr. R. J. LON
Miss MAUD BOYD, | Mr. CHARLES
Miss ALICE LETHBRIDGE, | AND
And Miss KATE JAMES. | Mr. FRED LES

The official programme for the 1892 FA Cup final between Villa and West Bromwich Albion at The Oval. A crowd of 32,810 saw Albion win 3-0 and afterwards the Villa supporters blamed their goalkeeper Jimmy Warner for the defeat by a team they had already beaten twice in League games that season (5-1 at home and 3-0 away).

In season 1893/94, Aston Villa won the League title for the first time. They accumulated 44 points (6 more than runners-up Sunderland) and won 19 of their 30 matches, scoring 84 goals and conceding only 42. Jack Devey top-scored with 20 goals, followed by Dennis Hodgetts with 12 and Charlie Athersmith with 10. Here are the players and officials from that excellent campaign: From left to right, back row: Mr Arthur Lees (director), J. Grierson (trainer), Mr Richard Cooper (director), Mr Josuah Margoschis (chairman), John Baird, Mr William McGregor (director, later to be chairman), Bill Dunning (goalkeeper), Jim Welford, Mr Frederick Rinder (director, later to be chairman), Mr George Dunkley (director), Mr George Ramsay (ex-player and then secretary). Front row: Willie Groves, Jas Cowan, Charlie Athersmith, Charlie Hare, Jack Devey, Dennis Hodgetts, Albert Woolley, John Reynolds, George Johnson.

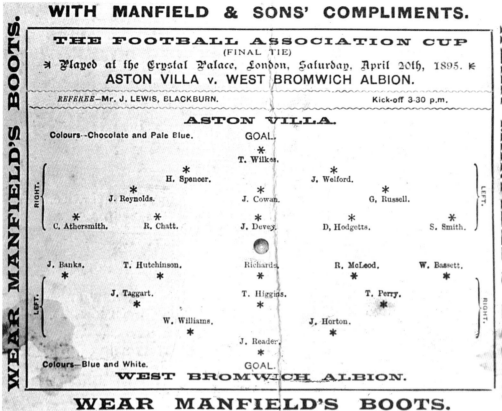

WITH MANFIELD & SONS' COMPLIMENTS.

THE FOOTBALL ASSOCIATION CUP
(FINAL TIE)
Played at the Crystal Palace, London, Saturday, April 20th, 1895.
ASTON VILLA v. WEST BROMWICH ALBION.

REFEREE—Mr. J. LEWIS, BLACKBURN.   Kick-off 3-30 p.m.

ASTON VILLA.

Colours--Chocolate and Pale Blue.   GOAL.
T. Wilkes.

H. Spencer.   J. Welford.

J. Reynolds.   J. Cowan.   G. Russell.

C. Athersmith.   R. Chatt.   J. Devey.   D. Hodgetts.   S. Smith.

J. Banks.   T. Hutchinson.   Richards.   R. McLeod.   W. Bassett.

J. Taggart.   T. Higgins.   T. Perry.

W. Williams.   J. Horton.

J. Reader.

Colours—Blue and White.   GOAL.
WEST BROMWICH ALBION.

WEAR MANFIELD'S BOOTS.

WEAR MANFIELD'S BOOTS.

Above: A programme printed for the 1895 FA Cup final between Aston Villa and West Bromwich Albion, when Villa gained sweet revenge for that 1892 defeat by winning 1-0 in front of a record crowd of 42,562 at the Crystal Palace. The only goal of the game was scored inside the first minute by Bob Chatt, with assistance from John Devey and, indeed, from the Albion 'keeper Joe Reader.

Opposite above: In season 1894/95, Villa claimed third place in the League table with 39 points. Everton (with 42) were runners-up behind Champions Sunderland (47). Besides winning the FA Cup, Villa also lifted the Lord Mayor of Birmingham Charity Cup (beating Small Heath 5-3 in the final), while the reserves won the Birmingham & District League title. This photograph was taken in August 1895 and features most of the players (in kit) who served the club so well during that campaign. From left to right, back row: Howard Spencer, Tom Wilkes (goalkeeper, with cap), Dennis Hodgetts, Jim Welford. Front row (seated): Bob Chatt, Steve Smith, John Reynolds, James Cowan, Jack Devey (hand on ball), George Russell, Charlie Athersmith, John Campbell. Seated on ground: Jim Elliott, George Kinsey.

Opposite below: During the night of 10 September 1895, the FA Cup (in possession of Aston Villa) was stolen from the shop window of William Shillcock, boot and shoe manufacturer, based at 73 Newtown Row, Birmingham, where it had been on display. The mystery surrounding the theft has never been resolved, despite many stories and claims! Villa were fined £25 by the FA for losing the trophy and a new one was made by Vaughton & Son, a Birmingham firm of silversmiths, whose founder, Howard Vaughton, had been a Villa player only a few years earlier.

FOOTBALL OUTFITS DIRECT FROM THE FACTORY TO THE PLAYER.

WILLIAM SHILCOCK is the Inventor and Original Maker of the lace to toe and McGregor Football Boots, and notwithstanding the multitude of imitators his Football Boots are STILL THE BEST. Every pair warranted made on the premises.

THE BEST OF ALL FOOTBALLS, THE McGREGOR.
The McGREGOR has the largest Sale of any high-class football in the kingdom, being used in the International Matches, League International Matches, League Test Matches, English Cup Finals, and the most important Cup Competitions in the Kingdom. Also by Aston Villa, Sunderland, Bury, Sheffield United, Sheffield Wednesday, Stoke, Wolverhampton Wanderers, Small Heath, Millwall Athletic, Woolwich Arsenal, Grimsby Town, &c., &c.   ROUND.   SOUND.   UNEQUALLED.

FOOTBALL SHIRTS.

BEST MAKE, SPLENDID QUALITY.

Direct from the Factory to the Player.

THE LEAGUE BOOT, Warranted,
Price 9/11, 8/11, 7/11, 6/11, 5/11, and 4/11.

The McGREGOR BOOT, Warranted,
Price 10/6 and 9/11.

The following are a few of the many Clubs whose players wore W.S.'s Celebrated Football Boots :—Aston Villa, Sheffield Wednesday, Glasgow Rangers, Derby County, Blackburn Rovers, Sheffield United, Sunderland, Millwall Athletic, Woolwich Arsenal, West Bromwich Albion, Wolverhampton Wanderers, Newton Heath, Small Heath, Burnley, Stoke, Bury, Grimsby Town, Celtic, Third Lanark, Hibernians, Ayr, Notts Forest, Luton Town, Leicester Fosse, Burton Swifts, &c.   Testimonials from over 40 International Players.

The MacGREGOR, price 10s.
Can only be obtained direct from the Patentee, WM. SHILCOCK.
The League Football..8s. 6d. | The Clinker Football..6s. 6d.
The Bulldog   „   8s. 0d. | The Starr   „   5s. 6d.
The Endurance „   7s. 6d. | The Jun. League „   4s. 11d

		EACH.	DOZ.
W.S. Indestructible Shirt		3/6	40/-
W.S. League Shirt, 2-in. stripes		3/3	36/-
W.S. „ „ Halves reverse		3/3	36/-
W.S. Junior League, 2-in. stripes		2/6	27/-
W.S. „ „ Halves		2/6	26/-
W.S. Shirts and Sashes		27/- and 30/- doz.	

Special Designs made to order in two days.
Football Knickers................from 1/6 to 3/6

FOOTBALL GOAL NETS, from 35s. to 60s. per Set.   STEAM TARRED AND WARRANTED.

As supplied to the Irish Football Association, Aston Villa, Wolverhampton Wanderers, West Bromwich Albion, Small Heath, and over 100 leading clubs last Season.
Boxing Gloves and Punching Balls, Belts, Gymnastic Suits, Swimming Costumes, Caps, Running Pumps (Dinneford's best Horsehair).
Flesh Gloves, 3s. 9d. and 4s.   Cyclists' Racing Shoes and Outfits, etc., a Speciality.
Price List, over 250 Illustrations, post free.   Buy direct from the Factory, and save Retailers' profit.

ONLY ADDRESS   **WM. SHILCOCK,** 73, NEWTOWN ROW, BIRMINGHAM.
Football Outfitter to Aston Villa.

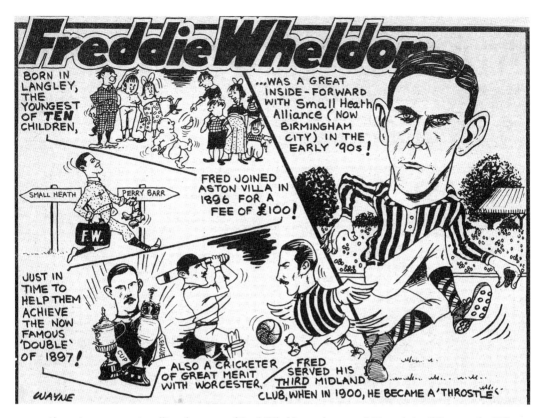

Above: A cartoon strip telling the story of Fred Wheldon, who scored 74 goals in 138 games for Villa between 1896 and 1900. He also played for England.

Opposite above: Two Aston Villa players, John Reynolds and Steve Smith, plus Jimmy Crabtree, who was later to join Villa from Burnley, helped England beat Scotland 3-0 in a home international match at Everton in April 1895, Smith (on 44 minutes) scoring one of the goals in front of 42,500 spectators. The photograph shows the triumphant England side. From left to right, back row: Mr Nicholas L. Jackson (official), Lewis Vaughan Lodge (Cambridge University), John Reynolds (Villa), John Reid (match referee), John Holt (Everton), John Sutcliffe (goalkeeper, Bolton Wanderers), Ernest Needham (Sheffield United), Jimmy Crabtree (Burnley), Richard E. Lythgoe (official), Mr Charles J Hughes (official). Front row: Billy Bassett (West Bromwich Albion), Steve Bloomer (Derby County), John Goodall (Derby County), Robert Cunliffe Gosling (Old Etonians), Steve Smith (Villa).

Opposite below: A boot, ball and shirt advert, which appeared regularly in the local Birmingham newspapers.

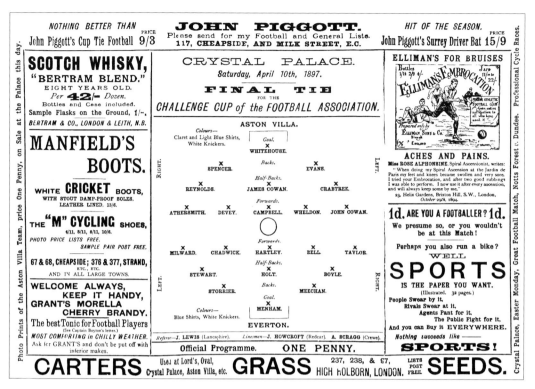

An official matchday card/programme for the FA Cup final between Aston Villa and Everton at the Crystal Palace In 1896/97, Villa emulated Preston North End's feat (achieved in 1888/89) by completing the double, winning the League Championship and the FA Cup in the same season. They won the League with 47 points (11 more than runners-up Sheffield United). Their best win (out of 21) was the 6-2 home victory over Bolton Wanderers. Fred Wheldon top-scored with 18 (out of the 73 League goals netted) and the average attendance at home games was 13,200 – the best in the club's history at that point. In the FA Cup, Villa knocked out, in turn, Newcastle United, Notts County, Preston North End (after two replays) and Liverpool, before beating Everton 3-2 in the final at the Crystal Palace. An epic encounter attracted a crowd of 65,891 and Scotsman John Campbell, Fred Wheldon and Jimmy Crabtree scored the Villa goals.

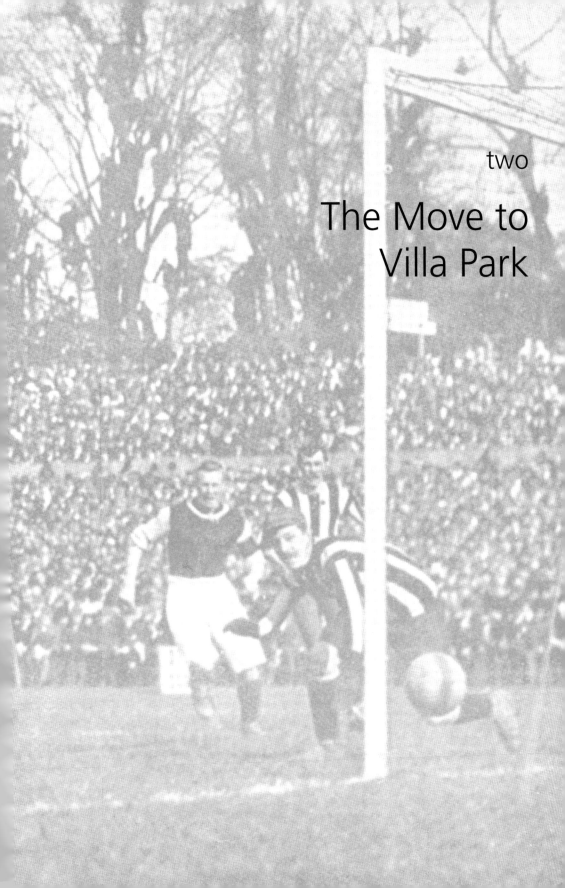

two

The Move to Villa Park

Above: Aston Villa moved to their present home, Villa Park, in April 1897, having previously played home matches at Aston Park, Wilson Road, the Aston Lower Grounds and Wellington Road. The Lower Grounds was a hive of activity for all sporting events during the last quarter of the nineteenth century and Villa played some matches there in the mid–1870s.

Right: A map showing the position of Villa Park and the surrounding area.

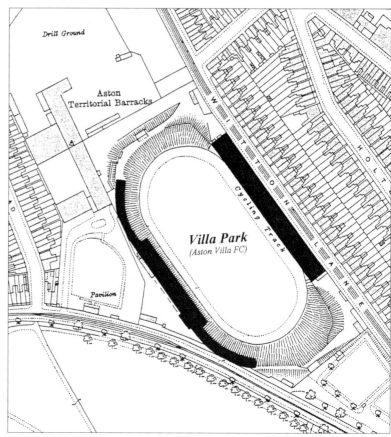

The Sheriff of London Charity Shield.

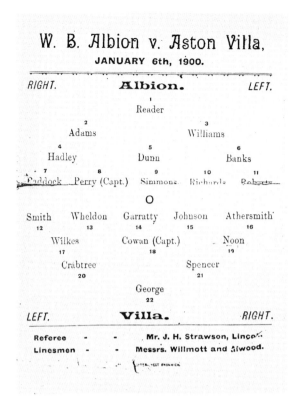

W. B. Albion v. Aston Villa,

JANUARY 6th, 1900.

RIGHT.   **Albion.**   LEFT.

1
Reader

2   3
Adams   Williams

4   5   6
Hadley   Dunn   Banks

7   8   9   10   11
Paddock   Perry (Capt.)   Simmons   Richards   Roberts

O

Smith   Wheldon   Garratty   Johnson   Athersmith
12   13   14   15   16

Wilkes   Cowan (Capt.)   Noon
17   18   19

Crabtree   Spencer
20   21

George
22

LEFT.   **Villa.**   RIGHT.

Referee -   -   **Mr. J. H. Strawson, Lincon.**
Linesmen -   -   **Messrs. Willmott and Atwood.**

On 6 January 1900, Villa travelled the short distance to play West Bromwich Albion in a League game at Stoney Lane. Going for their fifth title, Villa produced a dogged performance and won 2-0 in front of 6,575 spectators – Billy Garraty, later to join Albion, scored both goals. This is the match card from that local derby.

Action from Aston Villa's FA Cup semi-final clash with Everton at Stoke's Victoria Ground in 1905. There are nine Villa players in the picture as they defend a right-wing corner. Goalkeeper Billy George is on the far right, with full-back Freddie Miles in front of him. This game ended in a 1-1 draw, but Villa won the replay, in Nottingham, 2-1.

Villa's progress to the final of the FA Cup in 1905 saw them overcome Leicester Fosse (5-1), Bury (3-2) and Fulham (5-0), all at home, in the first three rounds. They ousted Everton in the semi-final (after a replay) and then, in front of a huge crowd of 101,117, they defeated Newcastle United 2-0 at the Crystal Palace to lift the trophy, thanks to two goals from ace marksman Harry Hampton. Here, Hampton opens the scoring on three minutes (above) and following Albert Hall's left-wing corner, Hampton has another effort scrambled off the line (below) as Villa press for a second goal before half-time.

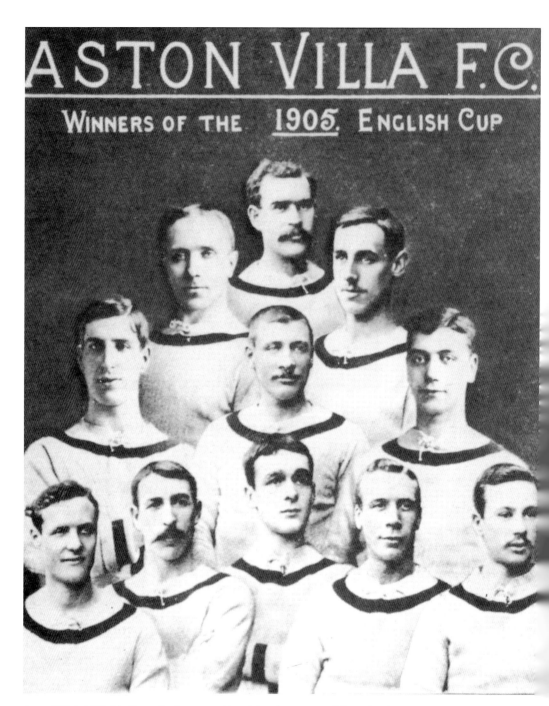

Aston Villa's 1905 FA Cup-winning team. Six of the players were full England internationals, namely goalkeeper Billy George, full-back Howard Spencer, centre-half Alex Leake and forwards Billy Brawn, Billy Garraty and Joe Bache. Later on, both Harry Hampton and Albert Hall were also to win caps.

The year 1906 saw the first-ever issue of the official club programme – *The Villa News and Record*. It was produced for the home League game with Blackburn Rovers on Saturday 1 September, when a crowd of 40,000 saw Villa win 4-2, with goals by Harry Hampton, Joe Bache, Joey Walters and Jimmy Cantrell. The programme (No. 1, Vol. 1) was printed by Colmore Press, Lionel Street, Birmingham, and was published by Aston Villa Football Club. Around 4,000 copies are believed to have been sold.

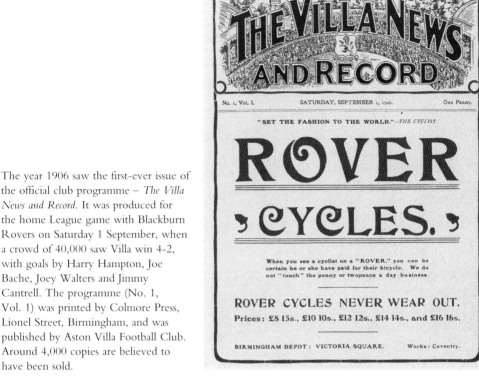

Howard Spencer.

With this issue of the Villa News we present a portrait of our Captain, and to do so affords us the greatest pleasure. It is almost unnecessary to offer any words of introduction. For a long number of years he has held a prominent position in the football world, and by his many good qualities he has gained the esteem of all lovers of manly and chivalrous sport. Without wishing to become fulsome, it may be honestly said that he has done as much as anyone to raise the tone of football, and has set an example of clean and straightforward play that has passed into common acceptation. For Aston Villa he has been a loyal and devoted servant, and it is fitting, in our opinion, that he should be honoured by the first place in our gallery of Villa photographs.

The Man of the Moment.

For to-day's matches in the First Division of the League, the following gentlemen have been appointed as referees :—

Aston Villa v. Blackburn Rovers ... Mr. T. Armitt
Bristol City v. Manchester United .. Mr. J. Adams
Bury v. Sheffield Wednesday .... Mr. J. W. Bailey
Liverpool v. Stoke .... Mr. F. Bye
Manchester City v. Woolwich A...Mr. H. J. Barker
Middlesbrough v. Everton ....Mr. F. Gardner
Newcastle United v. Sunderland Mr. T. P. Campbell
Notts County v. Bolton Wanderers Mr. J. B. Brodie
Preston North End v. Birmingham Mr. F. H. Dennis
Sheffield United v. Derby C. ...Mr. D. G. Ashworth

For Monday next, September 3 :—
Birmingham v. Bristol City ....Mr. J. T. Howcroft
Bury v. Woolwich Arsenal ....Mr. F. Heath
Derby County v. Manchester United Mr. R. T. Jones
Everton v. Manchester City .....Mr. F. Kirkham
Sheffield Wed. v. Newcastle U ...Mr. A. Kingscott
Stoke v. Aston Villa ....Mr. M. McQueen

For Saturday next, September 8 :—
Birmingham v. Newcastle United ... Mr. S. R. Carr
Blackburn Rovers v. Liverpool ...Mr. W. Nunnerley
Bolton Wanderers v. Sheffield U....Mr. T. Kirkham
Derby County v. Bury............Mr. J. H. Smith
Everton v. Preston North End......Mr. H. Pollitt
Manchester United v. Notts County..Mr. J. Mason
Sheffield W. v. Manchester C. ...Mr. J. T. Ibbotson
Stoke v. Bristol City ....Mr. C. C. Fallowfield
Sunderland v. Aston Villa......Mr. T. Robertson
Woolwich Arsenal v. Middlesbrough ..Mr. H. Ward

The Passing Breeze.

Bob Chatt has received the appointment of trainer to the Manchester City F.C. All will wish him success in his new sphere.

All good wishes to Harry Cooch and Harry Hampton on their joining the happy band of Benedicts.

All will be delighted to see Freddy Miles playing again. He has recovered much of his former robustness, and will, no doubt, be seen in the League team ere many matches have been played.

Albert Evans' leg has set exceedingly well, and, though yet unfit for playing, he is again in training, and will soon be on the warpath.

The bubble of the round robin has not yet been officially pricked, but the imagination of the individual who invented it has served him badly. There never was the slightest truth in it.

Billy Garratty (who, like the loyal servant he always has been, played many times last season with a weak ankle) has had to undergo special treatment, and is not yet able to turn out.

Our readers will join with us in congratulating Joe Bache on his much-improved form in the practice games. With no idea of individualising, it is pleasant to say so much of a valued servant, who, for no personal reasons, was more or less under a cloud last season.

Fred Wheldon has again been appointed captain of the Worcester City team. He looks as fit and well as ever. Mr. W. T. Miller, a well-known local sportsman, will fill the post of chairman. He has already done good service for football in the Faithful City.

True to Aston Villa "fortune," our brilliant forward, Albert Hall, has broken down in practice, and will not be fit for the first two matches at least. Tranter, the promising young half-back, has broken down, too. This is really the hardest of hard lines.

Birds of Passage.

Bowden leaves West Bromwich Albion for Southampton.
Elston leaves Aston Villa for Portsmouth.
Garratt leaves Aston Villa for Plymouth.
Hubert leaves Aston Villa for Plymouth.
Johnston leaves Aston Villa for Plymouth.
Kingsby leaves Aston Villa for Fulham.
Law leaves West Bromwich Albion for Watford.
Noon leaves Aston Villa for Plymouth.
Walker leaves Wolverhampton Wanderers for Northampton.
Kirby leaves Fulham for Birmingham.

ASTON VILLA v. BLACKBURN ROVERS.

ASTON VILLA.

RIGHT.   LEFT.

1—GEORGE

2—SPENCER   3—LOGAN

4—PEARSON   5—BODEN   6—CODLING

7—MILLINGTON   8—CANTRELL   9—HAMPTON   10—BACHE   11—WALTERS

○

12—DAWSON   13—BOWMAN   14—DAVIES   15—ROBERTSON   16—WHITTAKER

17—BRADSHAW   18—HOULKER   19—WOLSTENHOLME

20—COWELL   21—CROMPTON

22—EVANS

LEFT.   RIGHT.

BLACKBURN ROVERS.

Referee : T. ARMITT, Stoke.

Linesmen : A. AVERY, London. ; A. BOYCE, Stoke.

In the event of any alteration in the above teams, a board giving particulars will be sent round the ground.

ASTON VILLA Team for Monday—GEORGE, LOGAN, RILEY, GREENHALGH, BUCKLEY, CODLING, MILLINGTON, CANTRELL, HAMPTON, BACHE, and WALTERS.

Alex Leake also played for Birmingham and Burnley. His career spanned twenty years (1892-1912) and he appeared in 1,140 games for Villa and 221 for the Blues. He won five caps and was actually named as a reserve by England at the age of forty-one! Aston Villa's final game of the 1904/05 season was against Manchester City, who needed to win to become First Division Champions. A rough-and-tumble encounter, with skirmishes breaking out all over the pitch, ended with Villa triumphing by three goals to two. Afterwards, City's Sandy Turnbull was accused of punching Leake in the mouth and investigations into the circumstances went on until mid-August, when it was announced that Billy Meredith, City's flying winger, had attempted to bribe Leake with £10 to enable City to win the game. Meredith constantly denied the charge, but was suspended along with sixteen other City players, two directors, former chairman Bill Forrest and manager Tom Maley. The club was also fined £250.

Billy Garraty served Villa brilliantly for eleven years (1897-1908), during which time he scored 112 goals in 259 appearances. He was top marksman in the First Division in 1899/1900, won an England cap in 1903 and collected a League winner's medal in 1900, followed by an FA Cup winner's prize in 1905. He later played for Leicester Fosse, West Bromwich Albion and Lincoln City.

Above: Billy Brawn joined Villa from Sheffield United in 1901 and scored 20 goals in 107 games for the club, before transferring to Middlesbrough in 1906. He also played for Northampton Town, Chelsea and Brentford and gained two England caps.

Right: Fearless Harry Hampton – the idol of the supporters and a centre-forward with a never-say-die attitude – scored 242 goals in 375 games for Villa between 1904 and 1920. He then gave a good account of himself across the city with Birmingham. Also known as the 'Wellington Whirlwind', he gained a second FA Cup winner's medal in 1913, a League Championship medal in 1910 and four England caps. He also helped Blues win the Second Division title in 1921.

Left: Hefty goalkeeper Billy George (6ft 2ins tall, 14st 6lbs in weight) made 401 appearances for Aston Villa between 1897 and 1911, when he left the club to become a player-trainer at neighbours Birmingham. Capped three times by England, he featured in two League Championship-winning teams (1899 and 1900) and gained an FA Cup medal in 1905.

Right: Half-back Albert Wilkes hit 8 goals in 161 outings for Villa between 1898 and 1907. He won five England caps (1901/02) and played in the same two League Championship-winning sides as goalkeeper George. In addition to his spell at Villa, Wilkes also played for Walsall, Fulham and Chesterfield, later becoming a Villa director and a first-class photographer.

Action from the Chelsea *v.* Aston Villa League game at Stamford Bridge in September 1908. A crowd of 60,000 saw Villa win 2-0, with goals from Joe Bache and George Reeves, who also played for Barnsley and Bradford Park Avenue.

S. A. YORKE, PRACTICAL WATCHMAKER AND JEWELLER.
(Late with MARSH & CO.)

Watches and Jewellery of every description.

Magnificent Assortment of Articles for Presents.

Only Address—13, New Street (Opposite Grammar School).

FLETCHER'S CAFÉ, "The Caterers of the Midlands."
CORPORATION STREET.

The largest, most luxurious and up-to-date Café Restaurant in the Provinces.

Seating Accommodation, 800.   Afternoon Teas a Speciality.   Music All Day.

TEAMS FOR TO-DAY'S MATCH—EASTER MONDAY, APRIL 8th.

OLD VILLANS v. OLD HEATHENS.

Kick-off at 3.30 p.m.

OLD VILLANS.

RIGHT   LEFT

T. MASON (1)

H. SPENCER (2) or H. DEVEY   J. SIMMONDS (3)

T. G. PINSON (4)   F. BANKS (5)   H. BURCH (6)
or J. PEARSON   or J. BURTON   or J. WINDMILL

E. M. MITTON (7)   W. GARRATY (9)   H. HODGETTS (11)
T. BARKER (8) or R. DEVEY   or J. DEVEY   W. BAKER (10)

Referee : ALF. JONES or S. LAW.
Linesmen : Messrs. H. MORRIS and H. PITT.

F. HEATH (12) W. WALTON (13)   F. MOBLEY (14)   T. HANDS (15) E. FOUNTAIN (16)
G. LAYTON (17)   A. LEAKE (18)   J. DOHERTY (19)
A. GOLDIE (20)   F. STOKES (21)
W. C. ROSE (22) or IKE WEBB

LEFT   RIGHT

Reserves—J. WEETMAN, A. SMITH, H. SIMMS, C. R. HALL, H. MORRIS.

OLD HEATHENS.

N.B.—For Programme of Six-a-Side and Dribbling Contests, see next page.
For Teams, ASTON VILLA RESERVES v. WREXHAM, see page 571.
Also for Wednesday's match—GENERAL ELECTRIC v. AUSTIN MOTOR—see page 572.

☞ **Where to Dine!** "METROPOLE RESTAURANT"
Fletcher's, Ltd.
(FULLY LICENSED),
THE FRASCATI OF BIRMINGHAM.   35/36, HIGH STREET.
Luncheons, Dinners, Teas, and Suppers.
"Bass's Ale" only on Draught and in Bottle.   "Munich" and "Pilsener" Lager Beer on Draught.
The Ladies' Orchestra Plays Daily on the Balcony.

On Easter Monday 1912, a team of ex-Villa players (the Old Villans) took on their counterparts –
ex-Birmingham players (the Old Heathens) – in a challenge match at Villa Park. A crowd of 6,000
saw the men in claret and blue win a closely-fought game 4-3, Billy Garraty scoring twice.

Right: A Football League Championship medal.

Below: Notts County played their last match at Trent Bridge against Aston Villa on 16 April 1910, and a crowd of 13,000 were in attendance to see the visitors win 3-2, with goals by Charlie Wallace, Billy Eyre and Harry Hampton.

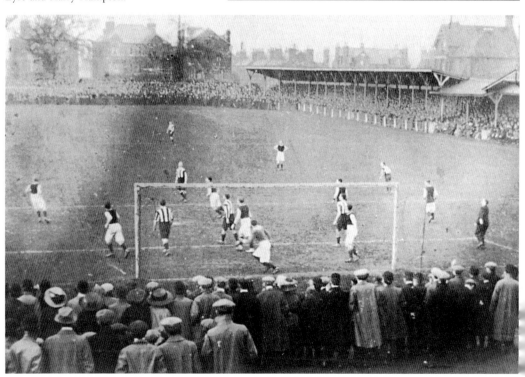

Clem Stephenson scored 96 goals in 216 games for Aston Villa between 1910 and 1921. He was then transferred to Huddersfield Town, where he became an even better player! During his excellent career he won two FA Cup winner's medals, three League Championship medals (all with Huddersfield, between 1924 and 1926) and gained one England cap (against Wales). Later, as manager, he guided the Yorkshire club to two more FA Cup finals (in 1930 and 1938).

Eight years after their FA Cup triumph over Newcastle United, Aston Villa met another team from the north east, Sunderland, in the 1913 FA Cup final, which was also played at the Crystal Palace. This time, with both teams in contention for the double, an amazingly large crowd of 121,919 turned out to see Villa win 1-0, Tommy Barber heading the all-important goal in the very last minute from Charlie Wallace's right-wing corner. Wallace had earlier missed a penalty. Prior to the game, Clem Stephenson, Villa's clever and instrumental inside-right, had told Sunderland's Charlie Buchan that had had dreamed the night before that his side won win and that Barber would head in the only goal of the game – an amazing coincidence!

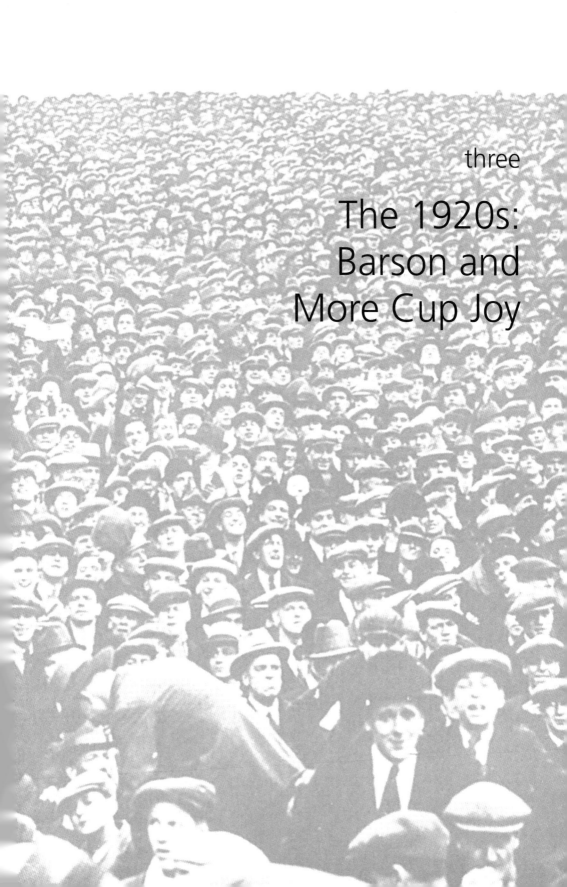

three

The 1920s: Barson and More Cup Joy

Above: Frank Barson scored 10 goals in 108 appearances for Villa, including one long-distance header against Sheffield United in 1921. He was also sent off at least twelve times during his career, but was nevertheless a wonderful player, who also played for Manchester United and appeared for England against Wales in 1919.

Opposite: The 1920 FA Cup final programme. Aston Villa, playing in the first FA Cup final to take place after the conclusion of the First World War, beat Huddersfield Town 1-0 after extra time. After making hard work of ousting non-League QPR (2-1), Manchester United (2-1), Sunderland (1-0) and Spurs (1-0), they had beaten Chelsea 3-1 in the semi-final at Bramall Lane. The final, played at Stamford Bridge in front of 50,018 spectators, was looking like a draw until halfway through the first period of extra time. Villa gained a corner on the left; Arthur Dorrell swung over the kick and the ball found its way into the net, more by luck rather than judgement, Billy Kirton's header deflecting off the Huddersfield centre-half Tommy Wilson. Villa's winning team was Sam Hardy; Tommy Smart, Tom Weston; Andy Ducat (captain), Frank Barson, Frank Moss; Charlie Wallace, Billy Kirton, Billy Walker, Clem Stephenson and Arthur Dorrell.

Billy Walker (right), seen here shaking hands with the Manchester City captain Jimmy McMullen prior to a League game at Villa Park in December 1928, made 531 appearances at senior level for Villa between 1920 and 1933. He scored 244 goals, including two on his debut in an FA Cup tie against QPR. A great footballer, he skippered the team for 6 seasons (between 1926 and 1932), scored 9 goals in 18 internationals for England and was an FA Cup winner, against Huddersfield Town in 1920, when only twenty-two years of age and still in his first full season with the club. Walker later managed Sheffield Wednesday and Nottingham Forest, whom he guided to FA Cup glory in 1935 and 1959 respectively. In 1934/35 McMullen was appointed manager of Aston Villa.

Eric Houghton in his playing days (left) and at the age of eighty (above). Eric was in the same Villa forward line as Billy Walker, and he, too, gave the club wonderful service, scoring 170 goals in 392 competitive games between 1927 and 1946. One of the greatest names in the club's history, he won seven England caps (between 1931 and 1933), played for the Football League, and helped Villa win the Second Division title (1938) and the Wartime League North Cup (1944). He left Villa Park for Notts County, and after managing the Meadow Lane club, he returned as Villa boss, guiding them to victory in the FA Cup final against Manchester United in 1957. He later became a director and president of the club. He was eighty-five years of age when he died in Sutton Coldfield in 1996.

Tom 'Pongo' Waring thrived on the service and crosses provided by colleagues Billy Walker and Eric Houghton. A long-striding, 6ft-tall centre-forward of sinew, muscle and bone, Waring was lethal inside the penalty area. Between 1938 and 1935, he scored 167 goals in 226 games for Villa, including a club record tally of 49 in the 1930/31 season when the team went goal-crazy with a total of 128, eventually finishing as runners-up to Arsenal in the First Division table. A crowd of over 23,000 saw Waring's first game in Villa's colours – a reserve fixture against Birmingham – and after that, he was a huge hit with the fans, but not with defenders! Waring later played for Barnsley, Wolves, Tranmere Rovers (his first major club), Accrington Stanley and Bath City and won five England caps. He died in 1980, aged seventy-four.

Huge crowds flocked to Villa Park during the 1920s and '30s, and here we see the packed terraces at the Witton Road end of the ground, when a record attendance of 74,625 saw Villa beat Walsall 3-1 in an FA Cup fourth round tie in January 1930.

A cartoon of the tie against Walsall, featuring Fred Biddlestone. The Walsall goalkeeper was soon to join Villa.

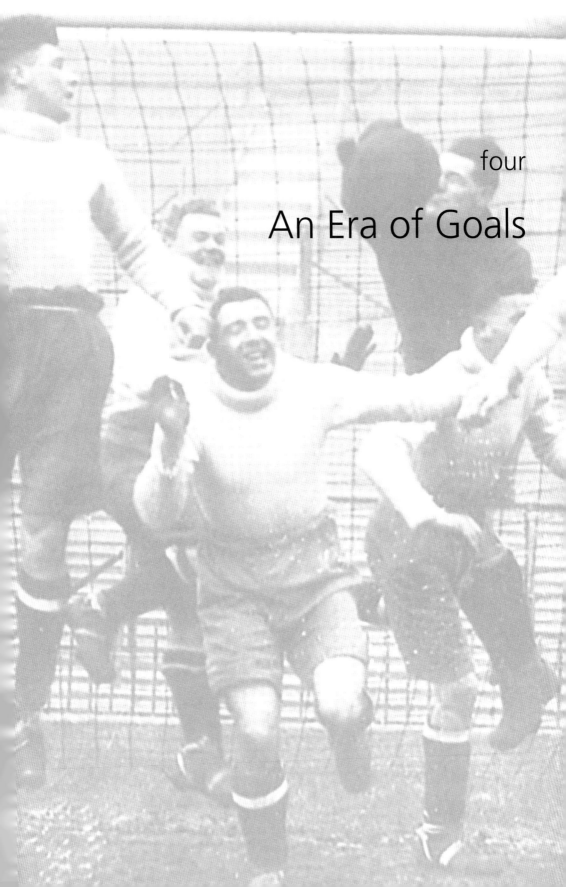

four

An Era of Goals

The Saddlers' goalkeeper Fred Biddlestone played so well in the FA Cup tie at Villa Park in 1930 that, a month or so later, he joined Aston Villa. He went on to appear in 160 games for the club before leaving in 1939. Biddlestone is pictured here between two of his Villa colleagues, full-backs Ernest Callaghan (left) and George Cummings (right).

AS EASY AS SHELLING PEAS

Individual Thrust—and Luck—Which Shattered Villa's Hopes

CHAMPIONS' GREAT TRIUMPH

ASTON VILLA 1, ARSENAL 7

1935 – Villa 1 Arsenal 7. For Aston Villa, the 1935/36 season was a complete disaster as they suffered relegation to the Second Division for the first time in their history. Villa won only 13 of their 42 matches and gave away 110 goals, with seven in a match being conceded on three occasions – at home against Middlesbrough, West Bromwich Albion and Arsenal. Ted Drake scored all seven goals for the Gunners.

The CHELSEA F.C. Chronicle

OFFICIAL PROGRAMME

of The Chelsea Football & Athletic Company, Limited.

MEMBERS OF THE FOOTBALL LEAGUE (First Division).
THE LONDON FOOTBALL COMBINATION.
Runners-up—FOOTBALL ASSOCIATION CUP 1914—1915.

VOL. XXVII. No. 6. Saturday, 19th September, 1931. TWOPENCE. POST FREE 3D.

PAY UP THE VILLA! By Bernhard Hugh.

The Pensioner doesn't expect to get much change out of the Villa in these hard times but he hopes to get some entertainment tax at least.

A programme from the Chelsea *v.* Aston Villa League game at Stamford Bridge in September 1931. A crowd of 56,000 witnessed a cracking game of football that ended in a 6-3 victory for the visitors, 'Pongo' Waring scoring four goals and Eric Houghton two.

ASTON

A F.C.

Previous page: These are the players who started that ill-fated 1935/36 season for Aston Villa, hoping for far better things than they actually achieved. From left to right, back row: Dennis Watkin, Tom Gardner, Jimmy Allen, Harry Morton, Jimmy Gibson, Billy Kingdon, Jimmy McLuckie. Middle row: Harry Cooch (trainer), Tom Waring, Dai Astley, Bob Brocklebank, Ronnie Dix, Joe Beresford, Jimmy McMullan (manager). Front row: George Beeson, Frank Broome, Eric Houghton, Arthur Cunliffe, Danny Blair.

Left: Bob Iverson was a strong, aggressive defender, who started his senior career with Lincoln City in 1934. He then played for Wolverhampton Wanderers and joined Villa in 1936. He remained with the club until 1948, when he retired, and during his twelve years with Villa, he amassed 153 competitive appearances and scored 12 goals. A self-taught pianist and jazz enthusiast, Iverson was only forty-three when he died in 1953.

Opposite left: Unfortunately, Bill Cobley's career was disrupted by the Second World War. He joined Villa in 1932 but didn't play again after the hostilities. A very confident full-back, he appeared in only 47 first-class matches, mainly as a replacement for Scotsman George Cummings, during his thirteen years with the club.

Opposite right: Ronnie Starling, a splendidly gifted inside-forward, joined Villa in 1937 from Sheffield Wednesday, with whom he had won an FA Cup winner's medal two years earlier, under ex-Villa star and then Owls manager Billy Walker. Formerly with Hull City and Newcastle United, Starling helped Villa win the Second Division Championship (1938) and the Wartime League North Cup (1944). He was capped twice by England (in 1933 and 1937) and scored 12 goals in 99 senior games for Villa. He died in 1991, aged eighty-two.

Above: Six Villa players enjoying life during a routine training session at the Witton Lane end of Villa Park in the late 1930s. From left to right: Eric Houghton, Jimmy McLuckie, Arthur Cunliffe, goalkeeper Harry Morton, wing-half Tom Wood and full-back George Beeson.

Right: Versatile forward Albert Kerr scored 4 times in 29 games for Villa, whom he served from 1936 until his retirement towards the end of the Second World War, following a hip operation. During the hostilities he also guested for Charlton Athletic, Luton Town, Northampton Town, Plymouth Argyle and Portsmouth. He was also a police reserve, served in the Royal Navy and played for a Malta XI!

Above: The versatile Harry Parkes, born in 1920, played in six different positions for Villa, but his best was at full-back. He had trials at Villa Park in 1935 and eventually turned professional in 1939 after a spell as an amateur. Over the next sixteen years, up to his retirement in 1955, he scored 4 goals in 345 League and cup games, while also making a further 134 appearances in wartime football. He was in line for a full England cap in 1946, but was injured against Derby and never got a another chance. He later served as a director at both Villa Park and St Andrew's, whilst also running his thriving sports shop in Corporation Street, Birmingham.

Left: Scottish international wing-half Alex Massie, seen here in Villa's away strip in 1938, made 152 appearances for the club over a period of ten years from 1935. He retired to become the club's first post-war manager, a position he held until 1950. Born in Glasgow, Massie played for Partick Thistle, Ayr United, Bury and Heart of Midlothian, as well as for teams in America, before moving to Villa Park for £6,000.

Above: Jimmy Allen joined Villa for £10,775 from Portsmouth in 1934 – after playing in the FA Cup final. He made 160 appearances, gained a Second Division Championship medal in 1938 and retired in 1944. Capped twice by England, he also represented the Football League, guested for Blues, Fulham and Pompey during the Second World War and later managed Colchester. He died in 1995, aged eighty-six.

Above right: Centre-half Tom Griffiths scored once in 67 games for Villa, whom he served from 1935 to 1938, when he was forced to retire. A Welsh international (capped 21 times) he played for Wrexham, Everton, Bolton Wanderers and Middlesbrough before moving to Villa Park. He died in 1981, aged seventy-nine.

Right: Ernie Callaghan made 142 appearances for Aston Villa between 1930 and 1947. Nicknamed 'Mush', he too helped the club win the Second Division title in 1938 and was rewarded with the BEM for bravery during the Birmingham Blitz in 1942. He died in 1972, aged sixty-two.

Left: Outside-right Jackie Maund spent five years at Villa Park (from 1934 to 1939), during which time he scored 8 goals in 48 senior games. He moved to Nottingham Forest and later assisted Walsall, retiring in 1950.

Below left: Frank Broome occupied every position in the forward line at some point during his twenty-one years in the game. He served Villa (from 1934 to 1946), Derby, Notts County, Brentford, Crewe and Shelbourne before retiring in 1955. Later manager of Notts County, Exeter and Southend, he won ten caps for England, helped Villa win the Second Division title and was a member of both the Wolves and Villa teams that lifted the Wartime League North Cup in 1942 and 1944 respectively. He netted 62 goals in 138 competitive games for Villa and died in 1994.

Below right: Jackie Martin was a utility forward who netted 22 goals in 53 first-class games for Villa between 1935 and 1949. He played initially for Hednesford Town and during the Second World War played for England against Wales, as well as representing the Football League, the FA and a British Select XI.

Above: In May 1938, not long before the Second World War, manager Jimmy Hogan took his Villa players on a three-match tour of Germany. Two of the games, the first and last, were won: 3-2 against a Select XI in the Olympic Stadium, Berlin, in front of 110,000 spectators; and 2-1 against a German XI in the Adolf Hitler Stadium, Stuttgart. The second game ended in a 2-1 defeat at the hands of a better German XI in Dusseldorf. This is the programme from the game in Stuttgart.

Above right: In August 1938, and again twelve months later, Villa played Midland neighbours West Bromwich Albion in two Football League Jubilee fund matches. Villa Park was the venue each time and the results were also identical, with successive 1-1 scorelines, watched by crowds of 26,640 and 16,007 respectively.

Right: Page 25 from the Aston Villa official handbook, showing season ticket prices for the subsequently void 1939/40 season.

Details of
SEASON TICKETS
for 1939-40.

NUMBERED AND RESERVED TRANSFERABLE SEATS (bearing holder's name)
in centre section of PAVILION, TRINITY ROAD:—
£4.4.0 each, including tax.

NUMBERED AND RESERVED TRANSFERABLE SEATS (bearing holder's name)
in Centre Section of OLD STAND, WITTON LANE:—
£3.3.0 each, including tax.

TICKETS admitting to the 3/- section
of the PAVILION, TRINITY ROAD, or the Centre Section of the OLD STAND, WITTON LANE:—
£2.4.6 each, including tax.

Application, accompanied by remittance, should be made to W. J. Smith, Aston Villa F.C., Ltd., Trinity Road, Aston, Birmingham, 6, or W. F. Dillingham and Co., Ltd., Travel Agents, 4 Church Street (opposite Grand Hotel), Birmingham,3.

—25—

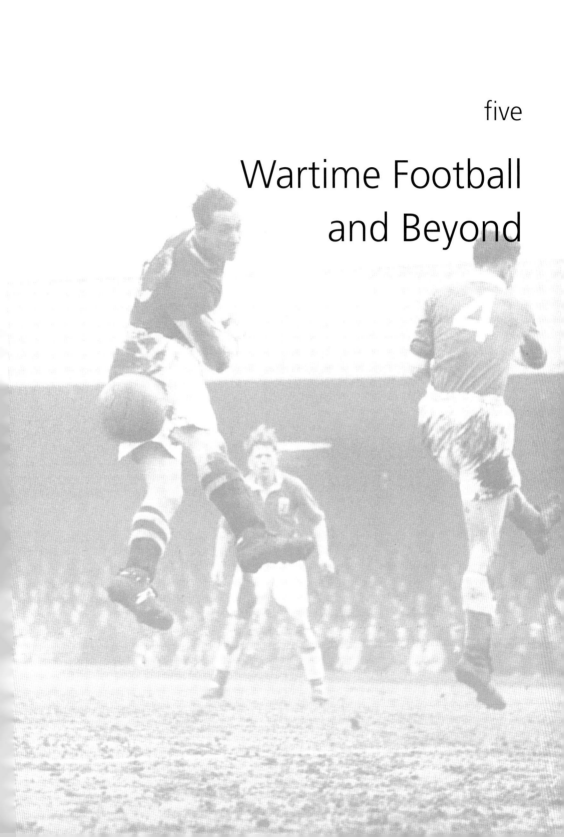

five

Wartime Football
and Beyond

Above: After some difficult times, both during and immediately after the war, League football settled down and the fans flocked to grounds all over the country, with Villa Park in particular attracting huge attendances, especially for derby matches. Here we see Billy Goffin (centre right) in action for Villa against Birmingham City in a First Division game at St Andrew's in April 1950. The result was a 2-2 draw and the late Trevor Ford scored both Villa goals.

Opposite: George Cummings, captain of Aston Villa (left), meets his counterpart, Fred Harris of Birmingham City, prior to the Football League South derby fixture at St Andrew's in January 1946. This game ended in a 3-1 win for Blues, who went on to pip Villa for the Championship on goal difference (96-45 against 106-58) after both teams had amassed 61 points.

Above: Villa's senior squad in the late 1940s. From left to right, back row: George Edwards, Eddie Lowe, Johnny Dixon, Keith Jones (goalkeeper), Frank Moss junior, Jackie Martin, Vic Potts. Middle row: Hubert Bourne (senior trainer), Dicky Dorsett, George Cummings, Alex Massie (manager), Bob Iverson, Albert 'Sailor' Brown, Phil Hunt (assistant trainer). Front row: Billy Goffin, Trevor Ford, Harry Parkes, Les Smith.

Edwards scored 41 goals in 152 League and cup games for the club; Lowe moved to Fulham; Johnny Dixon served the club from 1944 to 1961; Welsh international Jones played in 199 matches before switching to Port Vale; centre-half Moss appeared in 313 matches for the club; Martin guested for Spurs during the Second World War and Potts also played for Spurs and Doncaster Rovers.

Bourne was a former Villa player (1919-22); Dorsett joined Villa from Wolves, having scored in the 1939 FA Cup final; Cummings played in 232 League and cup games for the club; Massie was Villa's fifth manager; Iverson had just over 150 outings for the club; Brown was signed from Nottingham Forest after playing in seven wartime and Victory internationals for England and Phil Hunt was once a West Bromwich Albion reserve.

Goffin later played for Walsall; Ford was a £12,000 buy from Swansea Town in 1947; Parkes made 345 senior appearances for the club and later became a director; and Smith, an England international, also played for Brentford and was an FA Amateur Cup finalist with Wimbledon in 1935.

Opposite: Caricature sketches of Aston Villa players and officials from the late 1940s, drawn by the late, great *Birmingham Evening Mail*, *Birmingham Gazette* and *Sport Argus* cartoonist Norman Edwards.

THE VILLA NEWS & RECORD

Official Journal of the Aston Villa Football Club, Limited

Directors :
Mr. F. H. NORMANSELL, J.P. (Chairman). Mr. J. BROUGHTON (Vice-Chairman).
Mr. C. S. BUCKLEY. Mr. NORMAN L. SMITH. Mr. EDWARD SMITH.

President : SIR PATRICK HANNON, M.P.
Vice Presidents : Mr. J. E. JONES.
SIR PERCIVAL BOWER, M.B.E., J.P. Mr. ARCHIE BROWN. Mr. JOHN MORRIS, J.P.
Secretary : Mr. W. J. SMITH, Aston Villa Offices, Trinity Road, Aston, Birmingham 6.
Telegrams—"VILLA, BIRMINGHAM." Telephone—East 1646/7

| No. 28 Vol. 5 | FEBRUARY 28th, 1948 | Twopence |

VILLA'S EASY WIN.

Aston Villa, 3   Chelsea, 0
(Smith, Edwards,
Ford)

With the same team that won at Huddersfield, except that Dixon came in for the injured Graham, Villa had little difficulty in beating the Pensioners at Villa Park on Saturday last. On an icy pitch, and with a strong breeze blowing, Villa adapted themselves better to the conditions than did the visitors and if they had at least doubled their score it would not have been out of keeping with the play. Chelsea were rarely in the picture as an attacking force, and to their defence must be awarded any honours due to them. Medhurst in goal did much clever work and saved brilliantly at times, but it was Winter, with his three kicks off the goal line when all was lost, who saved his side from disaster. A lead of but one goal at the interval, scored by Smith in the forty-second minute, was but a poor return for all the good work done, but in the second half Villa were even better, they shot at every opportunity, and, what is more, were usually on the target. Shots were rained in at Medhurst from all quarters and from all our players except Jones, who was a starved witness of the game for most of the time. Our second goal, five minutes after the re-start, came from Edwards, and nine minutes later Ford got our third. We must again congratulate our players on their teamwork and zip, on a most treacherous surface ; they all did excellently, and it was not their fault they did not win the sweep, you can put that fault, if you can call it a fault, down to that man Medhurst.

Aston Villa : Jones (K.) ; Moss (F.), Cummings ; Dorsett, Parkes, Lowe (E.) ; Edwards, Dixon, Ford, Brown, Smith (L.).

Chelsea : Medhurst ; Winter, Bathgate ; Armstrong, Harris, Macauley ; Dyke, Bentley, Campbell, Walker, McInnes.
Referee : Mr. G. L. Iliffe (Leicester).

CENTRAL LEAGUE.

Huddersfield Town, 0   Aston Villa, 2

Having the worst of the play, on a snow covered pitch, last Saturday, the home side were fortunate to be on level terms at the interval. Villa still had the better of the game in the second half and two goals by Goffin gave them a well deserved victory.

Huddersfield Town : Clegg ; Bailey, Briggs ; Hunter, Bird, Watson ; Dickson, Doyle, Rogers, Reid, Hutchinson.
Aston Villa : Wakeman ; Guttridge, Vinall ; Chapman, Moss (A.), Iverson ; Smith (H.), Martin, Canning, Evans, Goffin.

BIRMINGHAM AND DISTRICT LEAGUE.

Aston Villa   1
Halesowen Town   5

Having the better of play on Saturday last the home side led at the interval by 3-1, the third one being by Morby, who put into his own goal. He however made amends just afterwards by scoring for his own side. Halesowen added two more in the second half and were good value for their win.

Aston Villa : McMillan ; Allcock, Atkinson ; Jones (R.), Morby, Millington ; Aldred, Clark, Haynes, Alsopp, Davis.

TO-DAY'S VISITORS.

To-day we have with us the famous and much talked of Arsenal, who, for most of the season, have been making the pace at the head of the First Division table, and seem destined to once again carry off the League Championship. Should such be the case it will be the sixth time the Londoners have taken League honours and they will thus tie with the record which Aston Villa have so proudly held since 1910. Arsenal won their first championship in season 1930-31 and they followed it up with further

Ansells
The Better Beer!

In February 1948, a crowd of 66,045 attended Villa Park to see Champions-elect Arsenal beaten 4-2 by an excellent Villa side. Johnny Dixon, Les Smith and Trevor Ford (2) scored the goals.

Left: In the 1948/49 season, Wolves won the FA Cup and finished sixth in the First Division. The two League games against Villa attracted an aggregate attendance figure of more than 103,000. There were 39,540 present at Molineux on Christmas Day to see Wolves win 4-0, and there were 63,572 assembled inside Villa Park for the return game forty-eight hours later, when Villa won 5-1 (Ford netting four times on this occasion).

Opposite: Trevor Ford – fearless, robust and exciting – scored 61 goals in 128 outings for Aston Villa between 1947 and 1950. During his career, he also played for Swansea Town, Cardiff City, Sunderland, PSV Eindhoven and Newport County. He gained 38 caps for Wales and was the first player to score over 20 international goals for his country. Sadly, Ford died in 2003 at the age of seventy-nine.

TREVOR FORD

YOUNG AND CONFIDENT, **TREVOR FORD** FIRST CAME INTO PROMINENCE IN **1945-6**, WHEN IN ONE OF HIS EARLIEST GAMES FOR **SWANSEA TOWN** HE SMASHED IN A HAT-TRICK FROM CENTRE-FORWARD AGAINST **ASTON VILLA**.

WITH **40** GOALS THAT SEASON HE WAS **TOWN**'S LEADING SCORER, AND **VILLA**, WITH GOOD REASON, PAID **£10,000** FOR HIS SIGNATURE NOT LONG AFTERWARDS....

ALREADY A WELSH INTERNATIONAL, **FORD** ENJOYED HIS SHORT STAY AT VILLA PARK, LEADING THE HOME ATTACK IN THAT GREATEST OF ALL CUP-TIES WITH **MANCHESTER UNITED** IN **1948**. 1-5 DOWN AT HALF-TIME, **VILLA** STORMED BACK IN HEROIC FASHION, ONLY TO LOSE GALLANTLY BY 4-6....

FORD ALWAYS MAINTAINED THAT SOCCER WAS A MAN'S GAME, AND WHAT HE LACKED IN SKILL HE MORE THAN ACCOUNTED FOR IN HIS RUTHLESS DETERMINATION TO SCORE AND TO SUCCEED.

IN OCTOBER **1950 £30,000** CHANGED HANDS, AND **FORD** LEFT THE MIDLANDS FOR A THREE-YEAR PERIOD WITH **SUNDERLAND**. ON HIS ROKER PARK DEBUT, TOUGH AND TENACIOUS **TREVOR** THRILLED HIS NEW FANS WITH A SUPERB HAT-TRICK OF GOALS....

GOALS WERE HIS MEAT AND DRINK, AND HE LIKED A CHALLENGE. HE WOULD POUND OFF AT TOP SPEED, HIS INTENTIONS WRITTEN ALL OVER HIM — AND RELEASE A CANNONBALL SHOT FROM ANY ANGLE OR DISTANCE.

FORD LOVED TO SCORE GOALS. IN TWO SEASONS OUT OF THREE AT ROKER HE WAS LEADING SCORER, AND IN A CUP-TIE AT **SCUNTHORPE** HE STRUGGLED ON AFTER BREAKING AN ANKLE — AND HIT THE WINNING GOAL!

ON THE DOTTED LINE, TREVOR...

IMPATIENT, HE COULD THROW ANY DEFENCE INTO PANIC, OR HARASS A GOALKEEPER UNTIL HE MADE A MISTAKE.

RESTLESS IN THE NORTH-EAST, UNHAPPY **FORD** RETURNED HOME IN **1953**, **CARDIFF** PAYING OUT ANOTHER **£30,000** FOR HIS SERVICES. HE AGAIN MARKED HIS FIRST HOME APPEARANCE WITH THE DECIDING GOAL.

HE WAS STRONG IN THE AIR, TOO, DARTING OUT HIS HEAD LIKE A SNAKE TO DIRECT THE BALL STRONGLY AND ACCURATELY TOWARDS GOAL. BOLD AND DANGEROUS, GIVING AND TAKING, AND RESPECTING NOBODY, **FORD** WAS IN EVERY GAME FROM START TO FINISH....

AFTER LEADING **WALES** ON MANY OCCASIONS, HIS FINEST HOUR WAS AT NINIAN PARK IN **1955** WHEN AT LAST HE STEERED THE 'RED DRAGONS' TO VICTORY OVER **ENGLAND** BY 2-1. FIERY, ENTHUSIASTIC **TREVOR FORD** CERTAINLY LEFT HIS MARK ON THE GAME.

...AND MADE SURE THAT THE OPPOSING CENTRE-HALF KNEW OF HIS PRESENCE, TOO!

Villa 'keeper Joe Rutherford pushes the ball away from the feet of Birmingham's Johnny Berry, later to join Manchester United. Villa centre-half Frank Moss looks on.

At the other end of the field, Blues goalkeeper Gil Merrick uses his elbow to keep Trevor Ford at arm's length. Home defender Ted Duckhouse is the player behind the Villa centre-forward.

Left: The former Everton, Middlesbrough and Luton Town player George Martin (right) was manager of Aston Villa from 1950 to 1953. He took over the reins from fellow Scot Alex Massie and, during his three years in charge, signed many fine footballers, including four Irishmen: Dave Walsh, Danny Blanchflower, Norman Lockhart and Peter McParland. Facing Martin in this photograph is Welsh international Ivor Powell, who started his career with Barnet. After serving Queens Park Rangers and guesting for Bradford City and Blackpool during the Second World War, he moved to Villa Park in December 1948, where he remained until July 1951 when he became player-manager of Port Vale. Powell scored 5 goals in 86 games for Villa.

Above left: Dave Walsh was a superb marksman, who scored exactly 100 goals for West Bromwich Albion before moving from the Hawthorns to Villa Park. He was signed for a fee of £25,000 in 1950 as a replacement for Trevor Ford. He went on to net 40 times in 114 games for Villa, who transferred him to Walsall in 1955, with Billy Myerscough leaving the Saddlers as part of the deal. Walsh, who scored regularly for Linfield in the 1940s, played in over 30 internationals for Ireland and helped the Baggies win promotion from the Second Division in 1949. He now lives in Thurlestone, south Devon.

Above centre: Peter McParland, scorer of 120 goals in 341 games for Villa, was one of the finest left-wingers of his generation. Fast, direct and lethal in the air as well as on the ground, he joined Villa from Dundalk for just £3,800 in 1952 and left for Wolves after ten years' service. He later played for Plymouth Argyle, Peterborough United and in America. Capped 34 times by Northern Ireland, 'Packy' was, of course, the 1957 FA Cup final hero (as far as Villa fans were concerned) and he also helped them to win the Second Division Championship in 1960 and lift the League Cup a year later.

Above right: Danny Blanchflower was a wonderful wing-half. He played for Glentoran and Barnsley before moving to Villa Park in March 1961, signed for just £15,000. After scoring 10 goals in 155 games for the club, he was transferred to Tottenham Hotspur for £30,000 in October 1954. As skipper of the London club, he won almost everything, including the League Championship, two FA Cup finals and the European Cup-winners Cup. He was also twice voted Footballer of the Year and took his tally of full international caps for Northern Ireland to 56. Blanchflower later went on to manage Chelsea. He was sixty-seven when he died in 1993.

Opposite below: Johnny Dixon, Colin Gibson, Miller Craddock, Billy Goffin and Les Smith – a very useful five-man Villa forward line – seen here during a training session at Villa Park. In fact, they lined up together on the opening day of the 1950/51 season, when Villa defeated West Bromwich Albion 2-0 at home in front of 65,036 fans. Dixon and Gibson were the goalscorers.

ASTON VILLA FOOTBALL CLUB LTD

W. J. SMITH
SECRETARY

SEASON 1953/4

W. E. HOUGHTON
TEAM MANAGER

A sheet of Aston Villa autographs from the 1953/54 season.

six

FA Cup Glory

Above: The Villa players face the camera for their pre-season photocall in August 1956. From left to right, back row: Peter Aldis (full-back), Bill Baxter (wing-half, ex-Wolves), Roy Pritchard (left-back, also ex-Wolves), Keith Jones (goalkeeper), Stan Lynn (right-back), Vic Crowe (wing-half), Peter McParland (left-winger, Irish international). Middle row: Bill Moore (trainer/assistant manager), the versatile Colin Gibson, Amos Moss (wing-half), Con Martin (defender), Eddie Follan (inside-forward), Johnny Dixon (ex-Newcastle United inside/centre-forward), Eric Houghton (manager, former Villa player). Front row: Tommy Southren (right-winger, signed from West Ham United), Ken 'KO' Roberts (young Welsh forward), Norman Lockhart (outside-left, ex-Coventry City, capped for Northern Ireland eight times).

Opposite page, top:

Left: Dave Hickson was a strong, aggressive centre-forward, who scored over 200 goals in a career that spanned fifteen years. During this period, he served Everton (two spells), Huddersfield, Villa (four months in 1955 – a single goal in twelve games), Liverpool, Bury, Tranmere Rovers and Cambridge City (non-League). He also managed Ballymena.

Centre: One player missing from the above line-up is centre-forward Derek Pace. He signed as a professional for Villa in 1949 and scored 42 goals in 107 games, before moving to Sheffield United in 1957, after losing his place in the side to Billy Myerscough. Pace went on to net 140 League goals for the Blades.

Right: Tommy Thompson lined up alongside Tom Finney for both club and country and, indeed, played in the same international match as Finney and Matthews for England, against Scotland in 1957. A goal-hungry inside-right, he joined Villa from Newcastle for £12,000 in 1950, and scored 76 goals in 165 games over the next five years before transferring to Preston, later assisting Stoke City and Barrow. He won two full caps, six years apart.

Right: Inside-forward Jackie Sewell cost Villa £20,000 when he signed from Sheffield Wednesday in December 1955. Already an England international, prior to moving to Hillsborough, he assisted Notts County, who sold him to the Owls for a then record fee of £34,500 in 1951. A clever player with an eye for goal (he scored 40 times in 145 games for Villa), Sewell remained at the club until 1959, when he left for Hull City. He later coached in Rhodesia and Zambia. He was twice a promotion winner with Wednesday (from the Second Division) and once with Notts County (from the Third Division (South) in 1950). He helped Villa to win the FA Cup in 1957.

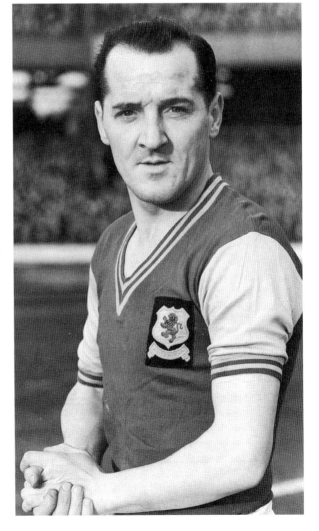

In the 1956/57 season, Villa went all the way in the FA Cup, despite not producing the goods in the League, and lifted the coveted trophy for the seventh time in their history by beating double-chasing Manchester United 2-1 in the final. After knocking out Luton Town, Middlesbrough, Bristol City and Burnley, they were paired with Midland rivals West Bromwich Albion in the semi-final. After a nail-biting 2-2 draw at Molineux, Villa won the replay at St Andrew's by a goal (Billy Myerscough) to nil and so entered their first final since 1924. Villa 'keeper Nigel Sims clears the danger from Albion's Brian Whitehouse in the semi-final replay.

Billy Myerscough, on his knees, watches his header beat Albion 'keeper Jimmy Sanders and left-back Len Millard, booking Villa their place at Wembley.

Above: Peter McParland scored twice to earn that 2-1 FA Cup final victory, but the final was somewhat marred when United's goalkeeper Ray Wood was taken off injured following a collision with match-winner McParland. Nevertheless, Villa played well for most of the game and deserved to win, although one must admit that if United had remained at full strength throughout the game (they had to place defender Jackie Blanchflower, brother of Villa's Danny, in goal), then things might well have been different. Here, Villa 'keeper Nigel Sims safely gets Tommy Taylor's effort over the bar, as Stan Lynn guards the line.

Previous page: Johnny Dixon is seen here leading out the Villa team (with eight-year-old mascot Andrew Pugh) for their 1957 FA Cup semi-final encounter with West Bromwich Albion at Molineux. He gave Villa seventeen years' loyal and dedicated service. Dixon joined the club from Newcastle in 1944, and by the time he retired in 1961 he had scored 144 goals in 430 games. It was Dixon who walked up the thirty-nine steps to Wembley's royal box to collect the FA Cup in 1957.

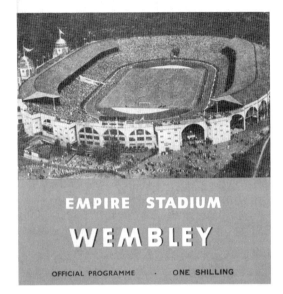

THE FOOTBALL ASSOCIATION CHALLENGE CUP COMPETITION

FINAL TIE
ASTON VILLA
v
MANCHESTER UNITED

SATURDAY, MAY 4th, 1957   KICK-OFF 3 pm

EMPIRE STADIUM
WEMBLEY

OFFICIAL PROGRAMME   ·   ONE SHILLING

Right: A programme for the 1957 FA Cup final between Villa and Manchester United.

Below: Autographs of the triumphant Villa players of 1957.

71

Above: In 1957, three teams from the Midlands – Aston Villa, Birmingham City and West Bromwich Albion – reached the semi-final stage of the FA Cup. Here, we see all three teams with their respective managers and trainers, photographed together at the M & B Sports Ground in Edgbaston, before getting down to business. Blues lost their semi-final against Manchester United, 2-0.

Opposite: Bobby Thomson failed to make the grade with Wolves, following his earlier excursions with Albion Rovers and Airdrieonians as an amateur. He netted 70 goals in 171 games for Villa between 1959 and 1963, when he joined Birmingham City. Thomson was a Second Division and League Cup winner with Villa. He ended his League career with Stockport County in 1968.

Above: A crowd of over 47,000 saw the Villa *v.* West Bromwich Albion League game at Villa Park in October 1958. Les Barrett gave Villa an early lead, courtesy of a mistake by the Albion 'keeper Clive Jackman, but after that it was all one-way traffic, as the visitors went on to win 4-1. Peter McParland claps his hands after Barrett's goal gives Villa the lead.

Opposite: Scotsman Ron Wylie, was a clever inside-forward with Notts County, and he continued to pull the strings in midfield when he joined Aston Villa for £9,250 in 1958. Seven years, 244 appearances and 28 goals later, he, like Bobby Thomson, moved across the city to sign for rivals Birmingham, retiring in 1970. He later managed West Bromwich Albion before returning to Villa Park, initially as a coach. He helped Villa win the Second Division title and the League Cup in successive years and played well over 700 games during his career.

After being relegated from the top flight at the end of the 1957/58 season, Villa quickly bounced back by winning the Second Division Championship at the first attempt. They also reached the semi-final of the FA Cup in 1959, only to lose 1-0 to Nottingham Forest (the eventual winners) at Hillsborough. Here, we see the players participating in pre-cup training on the coast. From left to right: Nigel Sims (goalkeeper), Jackie Sewell, Peter McParland, Ron Wylie, Vic Crowe, Leslie Smith, Jimmy Dugdale, Pat Saward, Billy Myerscough, Doug Winton, Gerry Hitchens, Peter Aldis, Johnny Dixon.

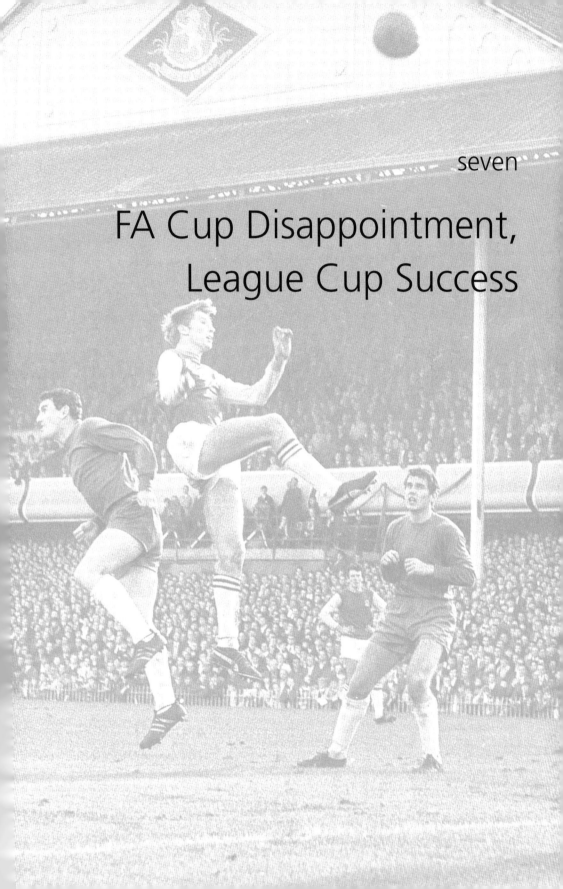

seven

FA Cup Disappointment, League Cup Success

Twelve months after losing to Nottingham Forest in the FA Cup semi-final, Villa once more suffered heartbreak when they lost 1-0 to Midland neighbours Wolverhampton Wanderers at the same stage of the competition at The Hawthorns in 1960. Here, Wolves' goalkeeper Malcolm Finlayson thwarts Villa's inside-right Bobby Thomson (ex-Wolves) with the Wanderers' skipper Bill Slater in between.

Vic Crowe looks on as Villa's goalkeeper Nigel Sims makes a flying save. Alas, his efforts were in vain, as Norman Deeley pounced to whip the ball past him for the only goal of the 1960 FA Cup semi-final clash with Wolves, which attracted an all-ticket crowd of 56,400 to The Hawthorns.

Vic Crowe, once an amateur with West Brom, appeared in 351 games for Villa (scoring 12 goals) between 1952 and 1964. He then moved to Peterborough United before returning as Villa's manager in 1970 (after a spell as coach in the NASL and at Villa Park). He won 16 caps for Wales and guided Posh to the League Cup semi-final in 1966. He was in charge of Villa for just under four and a half years, seeing the club slip in and out of the Third Division while also reaching the 1971 League Cup Final.

In 1960, the Football League Cup competition was introduced into English football. Aston Villa, the Second Division Champions, entered at the outset and they went on to win the trophy at the first attempt, although the final against Rotherham United was carried over until the start of the next campaign. After beating Huddersfield, Preston North End, Plymouth Argyle, Wrexham and Burnley (over a total of 10 matches), Villa beat Rotherham 3-2 on aggregate in a closely-fought final. The first leg at Millmoor resulted in a 2-0 win for United, but Villa stormed back to win the return leg 3-0 (after extra time), with goals by Alan O'Neill, Harry Burrows and Peter McParland. Here, the Villa players celebrate in the dressing room after their 1961 triumph. From left to right: goalkeeper Geoff Sidebottom, Harry Burrows, Gordon Lee, John Neal, Bobby Thomson, Jimmy Dugdale (standing), Vic Crowe (with cup), Jimmy MacEwan (standing), Alan O'Neill and Alan Deakin. Peter McParland was in the corridor doing an interview!

Manager Joe Mercer OBE spent five and a half years in charge at Villa Park (from December 1958 to July 1964). Here, he gives his pre-season team talk to the first-team squad in July 1962. Among those digesting matters are Derek Dougan (tallest, back row behind Bobby Thomson), Charlie Aitken (next to the Doog), Harry Burrows (arm on bench behind John Neal), Alan Deakin (in a relaxed, stretching pose) next to Gordon Lee (left) and Mike Tindall (right). Villa did moderately in the League in 1962/63, finishing fifteenth in the First Division. However, in the League Cup they again reached the final, but on this occasion were defeated over two legs by their arch-rivals Birmingham City, who won 3-1 at St Andrew's and forced a 0-0 draw at Villa Park. Ex-Villa full-back Stan Lynn starred for Blues, while Bobby Thomson and Ron Wylie were soon to move to St Andrew's.

On his day, Welsh international inside-forward Phil Woosnam was a brilliant schemer, who always found plenty of space in which to display his skills. Born in Caersws, Montgomeryshire, in 1932, he played in a single League game for Manchester City before dropping down the ladder to assist Sutton United and also Middlesex Wanderers. He signed for Leyton Orient in 1954, and after more than 100 outings for the London club, he switched his allegiance to West Ham United in 1958. He did very well at Upton Park, scoring 28 goals in 138 First Division matches before transferring to Aston Villa in 1962. He spent three years at Villa, during which time he appeared in 125 League and cup games and netted 30 goals. He was all set to become player-manager at Villa Park in 1965, but suddenly decided to quit the English scene and moved to America instead, joining Atlanta Chiefs. He later became commissionaire of the NASL (1969-83). Woosnam was capped 17 times by Wales (1959-63) and was voted the Amateur Footballer of the Year in 1956 after helping Orient win the Third Division (South) Championship.

Following Joe Mercer as manager of Aston Villa came Wolverhampton-born Dick Taylor, appointed in July 1964. A former centre-half with Grimsby Town and Scunthorpe United, he had previously been coach and assistant manager to Mercer at both Sheffield United and Villa Park. He held office until May 1967 and during his reign sold star striker Tony Hateley to Chelsea for £100,000 and spent £140,000 on new players – alas, it was to no avail as Villa were relegated at the end of the 1966/67 season. Here, Taylor sits with his squad prior to the start of his first season as manager. From left to right, back row: Alan Deakin, Gordon Lee (later to manage Blackburn and Everton), Bob Wilson (signed from Cardiff City), John Slueenwenhoek (who moved to Birmingham City in 1967), Lew Chatterley, Geoff Sidebottom (secured from Wolves), Mike Tindall, Charlie Aitken. Middle row: Dick Taylor, Jimmy MacEwan (an £8,000 buy from Raith Rovers in 1959), Stan Horne, Ron Wylie (who also switched his allegiance to St Andrew's and later managed West Bromwich Albion), Tony Hateley, Phil Woosnam, Harry Burrows (a dashing left-winger sold to Stoke City in 1965 for £30,000), Bill Baxter (trainer-coach). On ground: Alan Baker, Mick Wright. Messrs Deakin, Lee (although signed from Hednesford), Slueewenhoek, Chatterley, Tindall, Aitken, Horne, Burrows, Baker and Wright were all technically home-grown players.

Right: Most clubs during the 1950s and '60s produced a programme to cover two matches, Villa being among them. Here is a copy of the *Villa News* issued for home League games against two London clubs, Chelsea and Tottenham Hotspur in September 1963. For the record, Villa beat Chelsea 2-0 but were defeated 4-2 by Spurs. This type of programme is now becoming rather scarce, as three sets of collectors are seeking to buy them.

Below: Over the years, there have been some exciting contests involving Aston Villa and West Bromwich Albion. Here, Villa goalkeeper Colin Withers (once an amateur at the Hawthorns) turns a shot from Albion winger Dick Krzywicki over the bar during the clash in October 1966, when the Baggies won 2-1 in front of a crowd of 31,128. Villa's playing record (in League/Premiership competition) against their Midland rivals is interesting. The teams first met in 1888 and Villa's overall set of statistics now reads (to end of the 2002/03 season):

THE FOOTBALL LEAGUE - FIRST DIVISION
SATURDAY SEPTEMBER 14th 1963
CHELSEA
MATCH No. 7   Kick-Off 3.00
MONDAY SEPTEMBER 16th 1963
TOTTENHAM HOTSPUR
MATCH No. 8   Kick-Off 7.15

	P	W	D	L	F	A
Home	63	40	8	15	120	75
Away	63	19	16	28	86	99
Total	126	59	24	43	206	174

Left: Colourful, temperamental, eccentric, brilliant – Irish international striker Derek Dougan was all those, and more, rolled into one. He had an exceptional career, serving with Distillery, Portsmouth, Blackburn Rovers, Villa (from August 1961 to June 1963), Peterborough United, Leicester City and Wolverhampton Wanderers. Known as the 'lovable Irish scamp', the 'cheeky chappie' and simply 'Doog', he scored 261 goals in 692 appearances in competitive football, including 226 strikes in 60 outings for Villa. He was capped 43 times by his country and helped Wolves win promotion to the First Division in 1967 and the League Cup in 1974. He later returned to Molineux as chief executive (1982/83). The 'Doog' said he was proud to have played for Aston Villa. He's pictured here practising taking corner kicks during a training session.

Below: Dougan sneaks home a goal in a 4-2 win over Ipswich Town at Villa Park in 1963.

Above: An FA Cup fifth round tie between Villa and Wolves in season 1964/65 went to a third game before Wolves finally went through to the quarter-final by winning at the Hawthorns. Initially, a crowd of 52,101 witnessed the 1-1 draw at Villa Park. Almost 48,000 saw the replay at Molineux finish goalless after extra time and then, on a snowbound Albion pitch, Wolves played much the more controlled football to win 3-1 in front of 37,534 fans. Here, Villa inside-forward Barry Stobart, who started his career at Molineux, heads for goal as he gets in front of England international wing-half Ron Flowers and David Woodfield following a right-wing cross during the first game at Villa Park. Stobart scored 20 goals in 53 games for Villa and during his career he also played for Manchester City and Shrewsbury Town, later managing Willenhall Town and Dudley Town. He was an FA Cup winner with Wolves (against Blackburn Rovers) in 1960.

Opposite: Centre-forward Tony Hateley had a nomadic career. He served with Notts County, Villa (for three years between 1963-66), Chelsea, Liverpool, Coventry City, Birmingham City, Notts County (again) and Oldham Athletic and, in all, scored 211 goals in 434 League games. His record with Villa was 86 goals in 148 competitive matches. Strong in the air and an excellent target man, he amassed a career record of 211 goals in 434 League games and helped Notts County twice gain promotion (in 1960 and 1971), and in between times played in the FA Cup final for Chelsea in 1967 (when they were beaten 2-1 by Spurs – the team he scored four goals against in a thrilling 5-5 draw with Villa in London in 1966). Hateley's son, Mark, also played for Coventry City, as well as Portsmouth, Glasgow Rangers (two spells), QPR, Leeds United, Hull City and England.

Tommy Cummings was appointed as successor to Dick Taylor as Villa's manager in July 1967 and retained the position until November 1968. The former Burnley centre-half was in charge for just 60 matches, only 17 of which were won while 29 were lost. Here, Cummings sits with his team prior to the start of the 1968/69 season, but after seeing his side win only 2 games out of 20 (in League and cup) and drop to the foot of the Second Division table, he was sacked. From left to right, back row: Mick Wright, Colin Withers, Mike Tindall. Middle row: Bill Baxter (trainer-coach), Barry Stobart, Dave Pountney, Charlie Aitken, John Slueewenhoek, Lew Chatterley. Front row: Johnny MacLeod (ex-Arsenal) Brian Greenhalgh, Tommy Cummings, Peter Broadbent (another former Wolves player who played for England), Willie Anderson (a former Busby Babe signed from Manchester United).

In the summer of 1966, Villa Park was the venue for three matches in the World Cup. Here is a ticket for the clash between Spain and West Germany, which the Germans won by two goals to one in front of 45,187 spectators.

In 1967/68, both Birmingham City and Aston Villa were languishing in the Second Division, playing there together for the very first time, and both matches that season attracted large crowds. There were over 50,000 at Villa Park in October to see Blues win 4-2, and 45,283 fans assembled at St Andrew's in February to see Villa succumb to another defeat, this time by 2-1. This picture shows Villa's centre-forward Brian Greenhalgh winning an aerial battle with Blues' forward Geoff Vowden (who was later to sign for Villa) in the game at Villa Park. Also in shot, from left to right: Charlie Aitken, Malcolm Page, Willie Anderson, Barry Bridges, Brian Godfrey (wearing No.10) and Malcolm Beard (another future Villa player).

Here, Johnny Vincent, the Blues midfielder, tussles for possession with Villa's left-half Mike Tindall during the same match.

BIRMINGHAM CITY
(Shirts: Royal Blue; Shorts: Royal Blue).

ASTON VILLA
Shirts: Claret and Blue   Shorts: White

1	Jim HERRIOT	Colin WITHERS 1
2	Bert MURRAY	Mike WRIGHT 2
3	Colin GREEN	Charlie AITKEN 3
4	Ron WYLIE	Bob PARK 4
5	Winston FOSTER	Lew CHATTERLEY 5
6	Malcolm BEARD	Alan DEAKIN 6
7	Barry BRIDGES	John MACLEOD 7
8	Johnny VINCENT	Tommy MITCHINSON 8
9	Fred PICKERING	Brian GREENHALGH 9
10	Geoff VOWDEN	Brian GODFREY 10
11	Malcolm PAGE	Willie ANDERSON 11
12	Graham LEGGAT	John WOODWARD 12

TODAY'S REFEREE
Mr. N. C. H. Burtenshaw
(Great Yarmouth)

THE LINESMEN
Mr. C. L. Newsome
(Red Flag)
Mr. N. A. Lloyd
(Yellow Flag)

M&B

Your "45" Check

A	Scotland / England	F	Blackburn Rovers / Norwich City
B	Bolton Wanderers / Q.P.R.	G	Millwall / Derby County
C	Carlisle United / Portsmouth	H	Middlesbrough / Charlton Athletic
D	Blackpool / Rotherham United	I	Bristol City / Crystal Palace
E	Ipswich Town / Cardiff City	J	Huddersfield Town / Plymouth Argyle

Your "45" Check

K	Hull City / P.N.E.	O	W.B.A. / Fulham
L	Walsall / Scunthorpe United	P	Coventry City / Sheffield Wednesday
M	Arsenal / Manchester United	R	Sheffield United / Tottenham Hotspur
N	Newcastle United / Wolves	S	Nottingham Forest / Burnley

Best over the bar
M&B
It's Marvellous Beer
MITCHELLS & BUTLERS (MIDLANDS) LTD.

Above: A programme for the Second Division game against Blues at St Andrew's in February 1968.

Right: Brian Godfrey captained Villa on many occasions. A hard-working, resourceful inside-forward, who could also occupy the wing-half berth, he joined Villa from Preston in 1967 and scored 25 goals in 160 appearances before transferring to Bristol Rovers in 1971. Earlier in his career, he served with Everton and Scunthorpe United, and he later assisted Newport County and Portland Timbers and was manager of Exeter City. A Welsh international (three caps won), Godfrey was a League Cup finalist with Villa in 1971.

Tommy Docherty (after 29 days in charge of QPR) was appointed manager of Aston Villa in December 1968, but he remained in the proverbial hot seat for just over a year, leaving in January 1970 with his team struggling at the bottom of the Second Division. When he arrived at the club, Villa, to all intents and purposes, were in dire straits but somehow, perhaps more by luck than judgement, he guided them to safety, as they lost only 5 of their last 23 games despite not playing particularly well. However, he couldn't keep the momentum going and suffered the consequences. A Scotsman, born in Glasgow in 1928, Docherty played as a wing-half for Celtic, Preston, Arsenal and (briefly) Chelsea. He was then given the manager's job at Stamford Bridge (1961) and later held similar positions at Rotherham, QPR, FC Porto, Manchester United, Derby County, QPR (again), Preston, Sydney Olympic (twice), South Melbourne, Wolves (1984/85) and Altrincham, as well as taking charge of the full Scotland side in 1971. An FA Cup winner and finalist with Manchester United, he appeared in well over 400 League games and gained 25 caps for his country.

ASTON ViLLA NEWS & RECORD

SPECIAL MATCH 2

OFFICIAL PROGRAMME 5p   ASTON VILLA v SANTOS

INTERNATIONAL CLUB FRIENDLY   MONDAY 21st FEBRUARY 1972/ K.O. 7.45 pm

In February 1972, the world's most famous footballer, Pele, visited Villa Park with his club side, Santos of Brazil. A crowd of over 54,400 saw the friendly encounter, which Villa won 2-1.

Andy Lochhead – seen here with Garry Pendrey (Birmingham City) – was an aggressive striker who scored 54 goals in 154 games for Villa, whom he served between February 1970 and July 1973. Initially with Burnley, he was signed from Leicester City for £60,000 and, on leaving Villa Park, he joined Oldham Athletic, later taking over as coach at Boundary Park. He was an FA Cup finalist in 1969 with Leicester and a 1971 League Cup finalist with Villa, whom he also helped to win the Third Division title a year later. Lochhead, strong and competitive, was capped once by Scotland at Under-23 level.

Trevor Hockey was born in Keighley in 1943 and died in the same Yorkshire town in 1987. A wonderfully talented footballer, able to play as a direct winger or as an inside-forward/midfielder, he served in turn with Bradford City, Nottingham Forest, Newcastle United, Birmingham City, Sheffield United, Norwich City, Villa (season 1973/74), Bradford City, Athlone Town (player-manager), San Diego Jaws, San Jose Earthquakes and Los Angeles Quicksilvers. He managed Stalybridge Celtic and later coached the British Army soldiers' children's soccer team on the Rhine. His career spanned almost sixteen years, during which time he amassed well over 600 senior appearances (alas, only 24 for Villa, with a single goal scored). He played on all 92 League grounds in use when he was in action; gained nine full caps for Wales (via parentage qualification) and suffered the indignity of being sent off in his last international in 1974 (against Poland). He gained a Second Division Championship medal with Newcastle and helped Sheffield United win promotion to the First Division.

In season 1970/71, Aston Villa and Walsall met for the first time in forty years when they played each other in two Third Division fixtures. On 2 January 1971, a crowd of 19,203 packed into Fellows Park to see the first ever League meeting go in favour of the Saddlers by 3-0, Villa having a rare off day, as they were outplayed for most of the game. The two pictures here show two of Walsall's goals in their home victory: Colin Taylor's penalty (above) and Geoff Morris's cross-shot (below), which went in off 'keeper John Dunn's right-hand post. The player running in on the right is former Villa forward John Woodward.

Ian 'Chico' Hamilton, seen here in action against West Bromwich Albion, gave Villa excellent service, appearing in over 250 first-class matches and scoring 48 goals. Formerly with Chelsea (he was the London club's youngest ever player when he made his League debut in 1967 against Spurs at the age of 16), he joined Villa from Southend United for £40,000 in 1969 and remained with the club until 1976 when he moved to Sheffield United, later moving on to assist Minnesota Kicks (NASL). He played in two League Cup finals (in 1971 and 1975) and netted 65 goals in 308 League games during his career.

Sheet of autographs of Aston Villa players and officials from 1972.

A record crowd for a Third Division match – 48,110 – attended the Villa v. Bournemouth game at Villa Park in February 1972. At the time, both clubs were fighting it out for promotion and the Championship – and it was Villa who came out on top, winning 2-1 with goals by Geoff Vowden and Andy Lochhead. The BBC *Match of the Day* cameras were even present to film the action. This is the programme from that epic contest.

Villa won the Third Division title that season with an impressive record which read:

P	W	D	L	F	A	P
46	32	6	8	85	32	70

They finished 5 points clear of runners–up Brighton and Hove Albion and 8 in front of Bournemouth. Further down the table came Bolton Wanderers and Blackburn Rovers. Another bumper crowd of 45,586 saw Villa receive the Championship Trophy on the last day of the season at home to Chesterfield, whom they defeated 1-0, thanks to a goal by former Liverpool star Ian Ross – his first of the season. This is the programme for that last Third Division game, which is something of a collector's item these days.

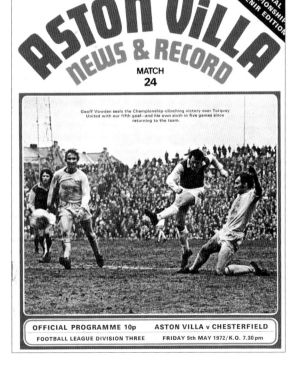

Left and below: In 1971, Jim Cumbes became the first goalkeeper for almost eighty years to move from West Bromwich Albion to Aston Villa (the previous one had been Bob Roberts in 1892). Formerly with Tranmere Rovers, he played in 79 games for the Baggies and added a further 183 to his total with Villa, whom he helped win the Third Division title (1972) and the League Cup (1975). He later assisted Portland Timbers, Coventry City and Southport amongst others. Cumbes was also an excellent fast bowler, playing county cricket for Lancashire, Surrey, Warwickshire and Worcestershire. He is now chief executive of the Lancashire CCC, based at Old Trafford. Here, we see 'Big Jim' tipping the crossbar (left) and in action against Ipswich Town (below), with Brian Talbot challenging.

Overleaf: Left-back Charlie Aitken served Villa as a professional for seventeen years (1959-76), during which time he appeared in a club record 660 competitive games (561 in the Football League). Born in Edinburgh in 1942, he made his debut on the same day Johnny Dixon played his last game for Villa (against Sheffield Wednesday in April 1961). He helped Villa win the Third Division Championship in 1972 and the League Cup four years later. He was voted Midland Footballer of the Year in 1975 and gained one Under-23 cap for his country. Aitken assisted New York Cosmos and Worcester City after leaving Villa Park. He was a great club man – one of the best.

eight

Saunders Arrives, More League Cup Success

Above: An official 100th anniversary certificate/poster presented to Aston Villa FC by the Football Association in 1974.

Opposite below: Here, Keith Leonard (No.9) beats his team-mate Chris Nicholl (No.5) and Albion 'keeper John Osborne to head home Villa's equaliser in the game at Villa Park in March 1975. Leonard popped up again later on to score his second goal, while Ian Hamilton netted the third.

There was more local rivalry between Villa and West Bromwich Albion during the 1970s, when both teams played together in the Second Division before rising to the First. The first time the clubs met each other in the Second Division was in season 1973/74, and it was Albion who came out on top, winning both matches – 2-0 at the Hawthorns, in front of 43,119 spectators, and 3-1 at Villa Park, when the turnout was 37,232. The following season, Albion again came out on top at the Hawthorns, winning 2-0, with Willie Johnston and Joe Mayo on target in front of a pre-Christmas crowd of 29,614. The return fixture at Villa Park attracted a crowd of 47,574, and this time Villa took the honours with a hard-earned (but well-deserved) 3-1 victory. Jimmy Cumbes, returning to his former club for the second time, gives away the first goal, allowing Willie Johnston's in-swinging right-wing cross to slip from his grasp and into the net. Joe Mayo (scorer of the second goal) and Chris Nicholl look on.

Frank Carrodus (in action here against West Bromwich Albion) cost Villa £95,000 when he was signed from Manchester City in August 1974. He scored 10 goals in 196 appearances over the next five and a half years before transferring to Wrexham for £70,000, later assisting Birmingham City and Bury. He gained two League Cup winner's medals (in 1975 and 1977), having been a losing finalist with Manchester City in 1974. He also helped Villa win promotion from the Second Division in 1975.

Opposite below: Goalkeeper John Burridge had a wonderfully varied career that spanned twenty-nine years from 1968. He played in turn for Workington, Blackpool, Aston Villa (signed for £100,000 in September 1975), Southend, Crystal Palace, QPR, Wolves, Derby County, Sheffield United, Southampton, Newcastle, Hibernian, Newcastle (again), Scarborough, Lincoln, Enfield, Aberdeen, Barrow, Dumbarton, Falkirk, Manchester City, Notts County, Witton Albion, Darlington, Grimsby, Northampton, Gateshead, Queen of the South, Blyth Spartans, Scarborough and Blyth Spartans (again, this time as player-manager). He also coached in China, at Leeds and at Newcastle. He made 915 appearances at club level (it was well over 1,000 if you count other matches), and his last outing was just before his 46th birthday, for Blyth, against Blackpool in the FA Cup in 1997. The effervescent 'Budgie' is the oldest player so far to appear in the Premiership – aged 43 years, 5 months and 11 days – for Manchester City against QPR in May 1995. A League Cup winner with Villa (1977), a Second Division Championship winner with Palace (1979) and a Scottish Premier League Cup winner with Hibs (1991), he also helped Wolves win promotion from the Second Division (1983) and made 80 appearances for Villa.

Above: Villa's 1975 League Cup-winning squad. From left to right, back row: Neil Rioch (brother of Bruce), Frank Carrodus, John Gidman (who went on to play for both Manchester clubs), Jake Findlay (later at Coventry City), Jim Cumbes, Charlie Aitken, Frank Pimblett, Chris Nicholl (who moved to Southampton and later managed Walsall), Keith Leonard. Front row: Ray Graydon, John Robson, Brian Little (later manager of Villa, as well as Wolves, Stoke and WBA), Ron Saunders, 'Chico' Hamilton, Ian Ross, Bobby McDonald (who went on to play for Manchester City, Coventry, Oxford, Leeds and Wolves), Jimmy Brown (who, in 1969, made his League debut for Villa against Bolton at the age of 15 years and 349 days the youngest ever first team player for the club).

Above: Here, we see a delighted Bobby McDonald with John Robson behind him, holding up their winning tankards as they acknowledge the applause from the Villa supporters in the crowd of nearly 96,000.

Right: Ron Saunders managed Aston Villa from 1974–82. He also managed Norwich City, Manchester City, Birmingham City (1982-86) and WBA (his last club), as well as taking charge of Oxford and Yeovil Town. As a hard-nut centre-forward, Saunders scored 220 goals in 455 senior games while serving with Everton, Portsmouth, Gillingham, Watford and Charlton Athletic. As a manager he guided Villa to their first League title for seventy-one years in 1981, having earlier twice lifted the League Cup (in 1975 and 1977). He also took Norwich and Manchester City to the League Cup final. A hard and strict man, when manager at The Hawthorns, he was responsible for selling Steve Bull to Wolves for 'peanuts'. 'Bully' went on to claim over 300 goals for the Molineux side, after Saunders said that his first touch was poor. Graham Turner, who signed him for Wolves and was later to manage Villa, thought that too, but added that with his second 'he scored'!

The second city giants, Villa and Birmingham City, recommenced League action against each other in season 1975/76, when each team won its respective home game – Villa by 2-1 (in front of 53,782 fans) and Blues by 3-2 (before a gate of 46,251). In the following two seasons, disappointingly for the Villa supporters, Blues completed the double each time, winning both fixtures by 2-1 in 1976/77 (when the turnouts were 50,084 at Villa Park and 43,721 at St Andrew's) and by 1-0 in 1977/78 (when the respective attendances were 45,436 at Villa and 33,679 at Blues). Villa finally broke the sequence of poor results with a double of their own in season 1978/79. Andy Gray scored the only goal of a tight encounter at St Andrew's in front of 36,145 spectators, and Gordon Cowans netted at Villa Park, where again Villa won 1-0 in front of a crowd of 42,419. These last two defeats helped send Blues into the Second Division. Blues goalkeeper Jim Montgomery and defender Garry Pendrey are pictured trying to thwart Villa striker John Deehan in the League encounter at Villa Park in October 1977.

Full-back John Gidman played for Liverpool as an apprentice before joining Villa in 1971. He remained with the club until 1979, making 243 appearances and scoring 9 goals. He then joined Everton and later assisted Manchester United, Manchester City, Stoke City and Darlington. He almost lost the sight in one eye when struck by a firework in 1974.

Midfield dynamo Dennis Mortimer scored 36 goals in 406 outings for Villa between 1975 and 1985. Prior to that, he had played for Coventry City (from 1967) and after a loan spell with Sheffield United, he left Villa Park for Brighton and Hove Albion, later assisting Blues before taking up coaching positions, first with West Bromwich Albion and then back at Villa Park. He skippered Villa to League and European Cup glory in 1981 and 1982 respectively.

Above: Ready for a long coach journey during the 1976/77 season are, from left to right: Andy Gray (on steps), Ray Graydon, Frank Carrodus (behind Graydon), Leighton Phillips, John Gidman, Chris Nicholl, Brian Little and goalkeeper John Burridge. The bearded Dennis Mortimer is in his seat, waiting to go!

Right: Striker Andy Gray cost Villa £110,000 from Dundee United in 1975 and was sold to Wolves for £1.15 million five years later. He switched from Molineux to Everton in 1983, returned to Villa in 1985 and had spells with Notts County, West Brom, Glasgow Rangers and Cheltenham Town before returning to Villa Park for a third spell as assistant manager and coach in 1991. All told, he scored 78 goals in 212 outings for Villa. He won a handful of medals with Everton, scored the winning goal for Wolves in the 1980 League Cup final and was capped twenty times by Scotland. He is now a soccer pundit for Sky Sport.

Above left: Gordon 'Sid' Cowans served Villa as a player for fifteen years in three separate spells between 1974 and 1994. He also played for Bari (Italy), Blackburn Rovers, Bradford City, Derby County, Sheffield United, Stockport County and Wolves, and amassed a fine record of 825 senior appearances during a wonderful career, including 528 for Villa (with 59 goals scored). He was capped ten times by England and helped Villa win the League Cup, League Championship, European Cup and Super Cup. He was one of the great left-sided midfielders of his era – certainly one of the very best as far as Villa supporters are concerned!

Above right: Striker John Deehan netted 51 times in 131 games for Villa before transferring to West Bromwich Albion for £424,000 in 1979, thus becoming the first player to move from Villa Park to The Hawthorns since George Harris in 1909. He later played for Norwich City and Ipswich Town before becoming player–coach of Manchester City, then taking a similar position with Barnsley before returning to Carrow Road as coach. He later managed Norwich and Wigan Athletic and was also assistant boss at Villa Park under Graham Taylor in the 2002/03 season.

Opposite below left: Centre-half Ken McNaught – strong in the air, positive and confident on the ground – made 260 appearances for Villa, scoring 13 goals, during his six years with the club (1977-83). He started out with Everton, moved to Villa Park for £200,000 and then joined West Bromwich Albion for £125,000. He later assisted Manchester City and Sheffield United, before becoming coach at Dunfermline Athletic and then Swansea City's assistant manager (albeit briefly). He was a League Championship, European Cup and Super Cup winner with Villa. His father, Willie, was a Scottish international.

In 1977, Villa Park was eighty years old and here we can see a packed Holte End during a League game against Sunderland in March of that year. Villa won 4-1 with goals from John Gidman, Andy Gray and John Deehan (2). The attendance was 34,458.

Above: The top deck of the Witton Road (North) Stand at Villa Park was officially opened in 1994. This part of the stadium was terracing until the 1970s, although seating was put in on a temporary basis for World Cup games played here in 1966.

Above: In the 1977/78 season, Villa competed in the UEFA Cup and after beating Fenerbahce (Turkey), Gornik Zabrze (Poland) and Athletic Bilbao (Spain), they met Barcelona in the fourth round. After the first leg at Villa Park had ended level at 2-2 in front of almost 50,000 spectators, Villa travelled to the Nou Camp for the second stage, but were beaten 2-1 in front of a crowd approaching 90,000. Dutch international Johan Cruyff played a major part in Barcelona's triumph. Here, the two captains, Johan Cruyff and Leighton Phillips, go through the formalities with the match officials before kick-off at Villa Park.

Right: A programme from the away leg of the UEFA Cup fourth round tie.

f.c.
barcelona
Programa Esportiu

35
PTS.

F.C.BARCELONA

Copa de la U.E.F.A.
F.C.BARCELONA–ASTON VILLA

Campionat Nacional de Lliga 1977-78
F.C.BARCELONA–U.D.SALAMANCA

nine

League Champions and European Cup Winners

Above left: Villa won the Football League Championship for the seventh time in 1980/81 under manager Ron Saunders. The race for the title went to the wire, with Ipswich pushing Villa all the way. However, the Portman Road club won only 2 of their last 6 matches (one of them at Villa Park) while Villa won 3 and drew another to take the star prize by 4 points (60 to 56). The Championship was clinched with a 3-0 home win over Middlesbrough on 25 April in front of more than 38,000 fans. The winning squad, from left to right, back row: Eamonn Deacy (signed from Galway Rovers), centre-half Ken McNaught, goalkeepers Nigel Spink and Jimmy Rimmer, David Geddis (ironically an ex-Ipswich player), Gary Williams. Middle row: Jim Williams (physiotherapist), Des Bremner, Colin Gibson (who went on to play for Manchester United and Leicester), left-winger Tony Morley, inside-forward Gordon Cowans and Frank Upton (trainer-coach). Front row: defender Allan Evans (acquired from Dunfermline Athletic in 1977), striker Gary Shaw, Ron Saunders, inspirational skipper Dennis Mortimer, right-back Kenny Swain (ex-Wycombe and Chelsea player, who later assisted WBA, Nottingham Forest and Crewe), striker Peter Withe.

Above right: Gary Shaw was a poacher of half chances, who scored 80 goals in 212 games for the club he served for eleven years from 1977 to 1988. During his career, Shaw also assisted Blackpool (on loan), BK Copenhagen, FC Klagenfurt (Austria) and Sheffield Wednesday. At Villa, he formed a fine partnership up front with Peter Withe.

Left: Striker Peter Withe had already served with ten different clubs (including Southport, Barrow, Wolves, Birmingham City, Nottingham Forest and Newcastle United) before becoming Villa's record signing at £500,000 in 1980. He scored 92 goals in 233 games for the club, including the winner in the 1982 European Cup final, before joining Sheffield United in 1985. He later served with Portland Timbers, Blues (again), Huddersfield and Wimbledon (whom he also managed, albeit briefly) and is now the national coach of Thailand. He gained eleven full England caps.

Villa and Brighton and Hove Albion met for the first time in 1959 (in the Second Division), but it was another twenty years before the teams faced each other in the top flight. Here, Brighton's No.4 Brian Horton gets in a header in Villa's 2-1 home victory in August 1979, when a crowd of 28,803 saw Allan Evans (penalty) and Tony Morley score Villa's two goals in reply to one from Teddy Maybank.

Des Bremner was a strong-running Scottish-born midfielder, who scored 10 goals in 227 games for Villa (1979-84). Previously with Hibernian, he later played for Birmingham City, Fulham and Walsall. He is now associated with the PFA.

Goalkeeper Nigel Spink played his part in Villa's 1982 European Cup final victory – after coming on as a very early substitute for the injured Jimmy Rimmer. That was one of 460 appearances he made for the club he served for nineteen years (1977-96). Signed from Chelmsford City for £4,000, he was transferred to neighbours West Bromwich Albion and later played for Millwall, before becoming a coach with Birmingham City, Swindon Town and Northampton. Spink was capped once by England.

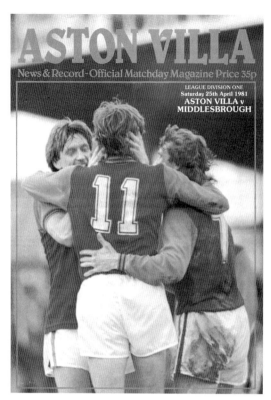

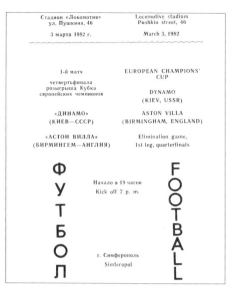

Villa clinched the League title with a 3-0 home win over Middlesbrough in April 1981. En route to reaching the European Cup final in 1982, Villa beat Dynamo Kiev and RSC Anderlecht (in the semi-final). They then took on and defeated the German Champions Bayern Munich 1-0 in Rotterdam.

Aston Villa and Stoke City – founder members of the Football League in 1888 – played each other regularly until the late 1980s, with Villa having perhaps the best of the exchanges overall, certainly in League competition. In season 1979/80, both clubs were in the old First Division (the Potters having just won promotion) and after Villa had won 2-1 at home in November, Stoke gained sweet revenge with a 2-0 victory at the Victoria Ground in late March. Here, we can see action from the latter game, wherein Paul Richardson's effort for the Potters strikes a post. Gordon Cowans races back to cover the goal as his 'keeper Jimmy Rimmer hits the deck.

In December 1982, Villa travelled to St Andrew's to play their arch-rivals, newly-promoted Birmingham City, in a First Division League game. Blues, who had won only one of their previous six matches, played exceptionally well and ran out convincing 3-0 winners. Here, Ian Handysides cracks in their second goal in front of almost 44,000 spectators. Sadly, following a brain tumour that spread to his spine, Handysides died in 1990 at the tragically young age of twenty-seven.

Andy Gray played for both Aston Villa and Everton during a fine career. Here, we see him in action for both clubs. *Above:* He jumps to get in a smart header for the Merseysiders in a League game at Villa Park in March 1985. The result was a 1-1 draw. Allan Evans (pictured second left) scored Villa's goal from the penalty spot, while future Villa player Kevin Richardson netted for the visitors. The attendance was 22,625.

Above: Midfielders Paul Birch (left) and Neale Cooper played together for Villa during the 1986/87 and 1987/88 seasons. Birch, more of a workhorse and forager, went on to appear in 219 first-class games for the club, scoring 25 goals, before moving to Wolves for £400,000 in 1991. He later assisted Preston North End, Doncaster Rovers, Exeter City and Hednesford Town. Cooper, a stern tackler and Scottish Youth and Under-21 international, was signed from Aberdeen for £300,000. He netted once in 22 outings for Villa before moving to Glasgow Rangers in 1991. After managing Ross County, he took over as boss of Hartlepool United in June 2003.

Opposite below: As a Villa player, Gray tries to get past Gary Stevens during the League game at Villa Park in April 1987. This time, Everton won 1-0 in front of a crowd of 31,218, and Kevin Sheedy struck the all-important goal.

In the mid-1980s, left-winger Mark Walters was beginning to show his talent. He joined the club as an apprentice, direct from the Holte Comprehensive School, and turned professional in May 1982. He took over from Tony Morley and, on his day, could be quite brilliant, his tempting, teasing runs causing defenders all sorts of problems. He went on to score 48 goals in 125 games for Villa up to December 1987, when he was transferred to Glasgow Rangers for £600,000. He later returned to England to play for Liverpool, Stoke City, Wolves, Southampton, Swindon Town and Bristol Rovers, announcing his retirement from top-class football in 2002. Altogether, he accumulated over 700 senior appearances, plus a handful of medals and England caps at full, Under-21 and 'B' team levels. Here, Walters is challenged by the Birmingham City full-back Brian 'Harry' Roberts during a Second Division game at Villa Park in August 1987 (above) and pictured playing for Glasgow Rangers (left).

Manager Graham Taylor, with midfielder Stuart Gray (left) and winger Tony Daley. Taylor had two spells in charge at Villa Park (1987-90 and 2002/03). He also managed Wolves, Watford and, of course, England. The versatile Gray appeared in 132 games for Villa (scoring 15 goals) between 1987 and 1991. He also played for Nottingham Forest, Bolton, Barnsley and Southampton (whom he also managed) and returned to Villa Park as assistant manager during Taylor's second spell at the club. Daley, a flying winger, served Villa from 1983-94, during which time he scored 40 goals in 290 outings. Transferred to Wolves for £1.25 million, he was plagued by injuries at Molineux, and after spells with Watford, FC Madiera (Portugal), Hapoel Haifa (Cyprus) and Walsall, he slipped into non-League football in 1999. Daley was capped seven times by England and helped Villa win the League Cup (1994).

Right: Warren Aspinall scored over 100 goals in 575 appearances at club level during a career spanning seventeen years (1983-2000). During that time, he played for Wigan Athletic (two spells), Everton, Villa (signed for £300,000 in February 1987), Portsmouth, AFC Bournemouth (two spells), Swansea City, Carlisle United, Brentford, Colchester and Brighton and Hove Albion. He helped Wigan clinch the Freight Rover Trophy, Carlisle win the Auto-Windscreens Trophy and Colchester gain promotion. He also struck 16 goals in his 50 outings for Villa.

Below: Defender Shaun Teale (seen here having a heated argument with the referee at Grimsby) spent four seasons at Villa Park, during which time he appeared in 181 first-class matches and scored 5 goals. Formerly with Weymouth and AFC Bournemouth, he cost the club £300,000 and when he departed he joined Tranmere Rovers for £450,000. He was later player-manager of Motherwell and, in 2003, he returned to Villa Park with non-League side Burscough, whom he helped win the FA Trophy.

Opposite below left: Left-back Gary Williams made 303 appearances for Aston Villa and accumulated over 500 appearances in total during his career. He served the club from 1976 to 1987 when he transferred to Leeds United, later assisting Watford and Bradford City. He helped Villa win the League, European Cup and Super Cup.

Opposite below right: Frank McAvennie, a Scottish international at Youth, Under-21 and senior levels, scored over 200 goals during his career – but made only three substitute appearances for Villa in 1992. He played a lot of his football north of the Border with St Mirren and Celtic, and also starred for West Ham as well as assisting Swindon Town. He helped Celtic win the double in 1988.

Above: Garry Thompson dives forward to score Villa's second goal in a 2-0 win over Manchester City at Maine Road in January 1988. 'Thommo' started his career with Coventry City. He then played for West Bromwich Albion (1983-85) and Sheffield Wednesday, before joining Villa in 1986 for a fee of £400,000. After netting 19 goals in 73 outings during his two years at Villa Park, he left for Watford and later assisted Crystal Palace, QPR, Cardiff City and Northampton Town. Manager of struggling Bristol Rovers for a while in 2000/01, his playing career comprised 614 senior appearances and 164 goals.

Villa and Stoke City locked horns in Second Division combat in 1987/88 and it was the Potters who came out on top, taking 4 points out of the 6 available with a 0-0 draw at the Victoria Ground and a 1-0 win at Villa Park. The two photographs here show action from the clash at Stoke in late October, when almost 13,500 were present to witness a tame draw.

Above: Lee Dixon (No.2), later to play for Arsenal and England, gets in a smart header as Steve Sims turns to see his 'keeper Nigel Spink make the save.

Right: Villa's Alan McInally (No.9) and Stoke's George Berry (No.6) participate in a first-half heading duel. Scottish international and former Ayr United and Celtic player McInally scored 28 goals in 72 games for Villa during his two seasons with the club (1987-89). He then tried his luck in Germany with Bayern Munich. Centre-half Sims also played for Leicester City, Watford, Notts County and Lincoln City, and made 47 appearances for Villa (1987-89).

There have been some wonderful contests involving Arsenal and Aston Villa over the years. Up to the end of the 2002/03 season, honours (in terms of wins and losses) are practically even out of a total of 148 League/Premiership matches and 17 cup matches between the two clubs. This picture shows goalmouth action from the League game played at Highbury in May 1987, when the Gunners won 2-1. Villa 'keeper Kevin Poole fists the ball to safety as a batch of players go for a header, among them the Villa duo of Martin Keown (later to play for Arsenal) and Andy Gray, with Tony Adams in the forefront. The attendance was just 18,463.

Above: Cyrille Regis started his Football League career with West Bromwich Albion, for whom he scored over 100 goals in seven seasons. He then joined Coventry and, after helping them win the FA Cup in 1987, moved to Villa Park four years later. After his spell with Villa, he then played for Wolves, Wycombe Wanderers and Chester City, announcing his retirement in 1996, with more than 200 senior goals under his belt. He also gained five full caps for England and represented his country at 'B' and Under-21 levels. In the picture above, Cyrille Regis (in the colours of Coventry City) sees defender Paul Elliott (Villa) get to the ball first during a League game at Highfield Road in October 1986. A crowd of 18,563 saw Villa win by a goal to nil, scored by former Sky Blues player Garry Thompson. Elliott's career was brought to an abrupt end in 1993, after he had accumulated over 300 senior appearances playing for Charlton Athletic, Luton Town, Villa (signed for £400,000 in December 1985 and remaining until July 1987), Pisa (Italy), Celtic and Chelsea. He was badly injured playing for Chelsea against Liverpool in 1992, following a challenge by future Villa player Dean Saunders. Elliott took Saunders to court, but lost the case and was subsequently faced with a legal bill of £500,000.

Opposite above left: Regis, playing for Coventry against Villa in March 1987, holds off a challenge from Chris Price. Full-back Price joined Villa in 1988 from Blackburn Rovers and returned to Ewood Park in 1992 after making 132 appearances and scoring twice. He also played for Hereford United, Portsmouth and Cinderford Town. He held the appearance record for Hereford until Mel Pejic, brother of Micky, surpassed it in 1991.

Above right: Centre-half Paul McGrath, seen here starring for the Republic of Ireland against Northern Ireland in 1988, won 83 caps for his country and played for Villa from 1989 to 1996, appearing in a total of 323 games and scoring 9 goals for the club. Prior to joining Villa for what was to prove a bargain fee of £450,000, he'd already appeared in 203 games for Manchester United, and after leaving the claret and blues, he went on to add more outings to his tally with Derby County and Sheffield United. He finally announced his retirement in 1998 with knee trouble which he had complained about for ten years! McGrath won an FA Cup winner's medal with United and two League Cup winner's medals with Villa.

Right: McGrath's international team-mate on many occasions was midfielder Ray Houghton, seen here in action for his country against Scotland in 1987. During a long career that took in West Ham, Fulham, Oxford United, Liverpool, Villa (signed for £900,000 in July 1992), Crystal Palace (from March 1995) and Reading, he played in 716 League and cup matches, notching 93 goals (netting 11 of them in 121 outings for Villa). He won 73 caps for Eire, gained two League Championship and two FA Cup winner's medals with Liverpool, and was a League Cup finalist three times, once with Oxford and twice with Villa.

Above: Dean Saunders had a very successful career as a top-level marksman. He turned professional at his home-town club, Swansea City, in 1982 and retired nineteen years later after serving Bradford City. In between times, he played for Cardiff City, Brighton and Hove Albion, Oxford United, Derby County, Liverpool, Villa (signed for £2.3 million in 1992 and remaining with the club until July 1995), Galatasaray (Turkey), Nottingham Forest, Sheffield United and Benfica (Portugal). He also gained 75 caps for Wales and netted 276 goals in 805 appearances for clubs and country. Surprisingly, he won only two medals, the first for FA Cup success with Liverpool in 1992 and the second with Villa for a League Cup final victory in 1994. His record as a Villa player was excellent – 49 goals in 144 outings. Saunders is now coach at Blackburn.

Opposite below: Striker Tommy Johnson started his League career with Notts County, who sold him to Derby County for £1.3 million in 1992. From there he switched to Villa Park (signed for £1.45 million in January 1995) and in March 1997, a fee of £2.4 million took him to Celtic. Johnson later played for Everton, Sheffield Wednesday, Kilmarnock and Gillingham. An England Under-21 international, he scored 17 goals in 71 appearances during his two years with Villa.

Above: Yugoslavian international midfielder Sasa Curcic cost £4 million when signed from Crystal Palace in August 1996. When he returned to Selhurst Park eighteen months later – having scored once in 34 games for Villa – the fee involved was just £1 million. Initially with Partizan Belgrade, he played for Bolton Wanderers before joining Palace in 1995, and later assisted New Jersey Metros (1999) and Tranmere Rovers (2000).

Above: Oxford-born central defender Martin Keown made his Football League debut for Arsenal. After a loan spell with Brighton and Hove Albion, he joined Villa for £200,000 in 1986 and, over the next 3 seasons, appeared in 133 first-class matches and scored 3 goals before transferring to Everton for £750,000. Three and a half years later, in February 1993, he returned to Highbury for £2 million and now, ten years on, he is still with the Gunners, having accumulated a career record of more than 700 senior appearances. Capped over 40 times by England, he has also represented his country at Youth, 'B' and Under-21 levels, and has two Premiership and two FA Cup-winner's medals to his credit.

David Platt.

From Player to Manager

These four men played for Aston Villa and later became football club managers, two of them (Gregory and Little) back at Villa Park. Gregory also managed Derby County; Little has had spells in charge of Darlington, Wolves, West Bromwich Albion, Leicester City, Stoke City, Hull City and Tranmere Rovers; McMahon has bossed Blackpool and Swindon Town; and Nicholl has been in charge of Southampton and Walsall.

Above: John Gregory.
Below: Steve McMahon.

Above: Brian Little.
Below: Chris Nicholl.

The Merseyside Connection

Over the years, several players have been associated with Villa as well as one of the major clubs on Merseyside – Everton or Liverpool. Here are four with that Mersey connection.

Above: Republic of Ireland international Steve Staunton (Villa and Liverpool).

Above: Striker Stan Collymore (Villa and Liverpool).

Below: Frenchman David Ginola (Villa and Everton).

Below: The versatile Steve Watson (Villa and Everton).